NEW YORK YANKEES

THEN & NOW

Thunder Bay Press
An imprint of the Baker & Taylor Publishing Group
10350 Barnes Canyon Road, San Diego, CA 92121
www.thunderbaybooks.com

Produced by Salamander Books, an imprint of Anova Books Ltd.
10 Southcombe Street, London W14 0RA, UK

"Then and Now" is a registered trademark of Anova Books Ltd.

Library of Congress Cataloging-in-Publication Data

Rossman, Larry.
  New York Yankees then and now / Larry Rossman.
       pages cm
  Summary: "A look at the New York Yankees through the decades, from their founding in the 19th century to the present. Includes sections on the history of the team and its stadiums, memorable moments, and the greatest players to don the team's uniform"-- Provided by publisher.
  ISBN 978-1-60710-807-8 (hardback) -- ISBN 1-60710-807-0 ()
1. New York Yankees (Baseball team)--History. I. Title.
  GV875.N4R675 2013
  796.357'64097471--dc23
                   2012045022

Printed in China

1 2 3 4 5 17 16 15 14 13

Dedications
To my beautiful wife, Amy, who lets me keep my Yankee chair from the old Yankee Stadium in our living room. I couldn't manage without you. To my sons, Jonathan and Zachary, for all the fun and laughter—you are my best friends. To my parents, Rhoda and Paul Rossman, for their love and support. Thank you Dad, for taking me to my first Yankee game. To my sister, Ellen, for playing Name That Yankee with me when we were kids. To my grandfather, Max J. Sommers, who loved the game of baseball.

Acknowledgments
Michael Heatley, for the opportunity and new friendship. Jeff Tamarkin, friends since 7th grade—thanks for the recommendation. Mike Bauch, my little league buddy and friend. Pete Citrin, my brother from another mother and for all the Yankee trivia in his head. Seymour Goldstein, a New York Met fan who I have been trying to convert for 20 years. Ted Green, who went with me to every Yankee game when we were kids. Jesse Goldberg, my baseball card guru. Louis "Duke" Weitzman—who actually saw Babe Ruth, Lou Gehrig, and all the Yankee greats— for all the stories he told me.

Additional research by Michael Heatley, Graham Betts, and Mike Gent.

Picture Credits
Library of Congress: pages 8, 9, 10, 11, 12, 13, 14, 16, 17, 19, 20, 21, 22, 24, 25 (top), 30, 31 (bottom), 39 (bottom right), 40, 50, 57 (bottom), 72, 75 (bottom left), 77, 86, 87 (top), and 109 (top).

Getty Images: pages, 15, 18, 19 (left), 27 (top left), 27 (bottom right), 31 (top right), 37 (top), 39, 43 (top), 44 (left), 44 (bottom), 47 (top), 48 (bottom), 51, 52, 53 (top right), 54, 55 (left), 59, 63, 64, 65 (top right), 67 (top), 69 (bottom left), 69 (bottom right), 71 (left), 75 (bottom right), 76, 79 (top right), 79 (bottom right), 81, 82, 84 (left), 85 (bottom), 89 (left), 90 (left), 90 (top), 91, 92, 94, 99 (bottom center), 100, 102, 103, 105, 106, 107, 110 (top), 111 (top left), 111 (top right), 113, 114, 115, 118, 119, 122, 123 (bottom), 124, 125, 126, 129 (top), 130, 131, 133 (right), 134 (top), 134 (bottom center), 135, 136, 137 (left), 138, 140, 142, and 143.

Corbis Images: pages 22, 25 (bottom), 26, 27 (top right), 28, 29, 32, 33, 34, 36, 37 (bottom), 38, 42, 43 (bottom), 44 (top), 45 (top), 46, 47 (bottom), 48 (top), 49, 53 (top left), 53 (bottom right), 53 (bottom left), 55 (right), 56, 57 (top), 58, 60, 61, 63, 65 (top left), 65 (bottom), 66, 67 (bottom), 68, 70, 74, 78, 79 (top left), 79 (center left), 80, 84 (right), 85 (left), 85 (right), 87 (bottom), 88, 89 (right), 90 (bottom), 93, 95, 96, 98, 99 (bottom right), 101, 104, 108, 109 (bottom), 110, 111 (bottom left), 111 (bottom center), 112, 116, 117, 120, 121, 123 (top), 127, 128, 129 (bottom left), 129 (bottom right), 132, 133 (bottom), 134 (bottom right), 137 (right), 139, and 141.

All "now" photography in 2012 by David Watts.

NEW YORK YANKEES

THEN & NOW

EDITED BY LARRY ROSSMAN

THUNDER BAY
P·R·E·S·S

San Diego, California

NEW YORK YANKEES

THEN & NOW INTRODUCTION

The Yankees celebrated their hundredth season in New York in 2002 by retaining the American League East title, finishing with a record of 103-58, 10 1/2 games ahead of old rivals the Boston Red Sox.

The centenary season afforded the opportunity to look back and to reflect how much the world's favorite baseball team—and indeed, the game in general—had changed since the franchise relocated from Baltimore and the Highlanders, as they were then known, took up residence in Hilltop Park.

Little, of course, has stayed constant since then: Yankee Stadium, constructed in less than a year, became their home at the start of the Twenties. It was known as 'The House that Ruth built,' in deference to their first superstar Babe Ruth. Its opening in 1923 contrasts with the unveiling of the Yankees' current home in 2009 right across the street from its predecessor.

Players' salaries have been an often-discussed topic over the years, with the Yankees as usual having the highest payroll in baseball. The salary total for 2002 had almost trebled since 1994,

2002 had almost tripled since 1994, amounting to $126 million for the full roster. At that time, Derek Jeter was the top earner at $14.5 million, but by 2012 he had been surpassed by Alex Rodriguez ($30 million), C. C. Sabathia ($24.3 million), and Mark Teixeira ($23.1 million).

Baseball players have always been well rewarded, their earnings typically exceeding those of the average worker by a factor of ten. In 1903 star player "Happy" Jack Chesbro was paid $5,000 while other players might have expected to command a salary of $2,000 to 3,000, but such information was not public knowledge back then. In 1930 Babe Ruth's yearly salary was $80,000 (the equivalent of $1.1 million today). When Ruth was asked how he felt about being paid more than President Hoover's salary of $75,000, his response was, "I had a better year than Hoover."

Wages are not the only thing to have risen dramatically since the Yankees' first season in New York. Attendances had also climbed from the early days when the average crowd at Hilltop Park was 3,115 and the total number of fans attending through the season was 211,808,

which was 80,000 below the average for the American League as a whole. The most-watched team back then was the Yankees' neighbors, the New York Giants, with an average of 8,279 and a total of 579,530. By contrast, in 2012, 3,542,406 fans flocked though the gates of Yankee Stadium, an average of 43,733 per game.

This book highlights many of the different sights that have greeted Yankees fans since 1902. Although ticker tape has been supplanted by shredded paper, the team has continued to enjoy more than its fair share of victory parades. Famous fans still flock to see the Yankees in action, but Jackie Coogan and Perry Como have been replaced by the likes of Paul Simon and Sarah Jessica Parker.

That fan following, of course, extends worldwide. Baseball may be a sport steeped in tradition, but the next chapters of the New York Yankees' story may well be written by Japanese players like Hiroki Kuroda. His recent recruitment by the Yankees has already helped cement the team's popularity in Asia, and more stars from the region are likely to make their presence felt in Yankee Stadium in the future.

Our pictorial coverage is worth more than a thousand words, illustrating how the game and the lifestyles of the men who play it have changed. But other things have remained constant. Wearing the Yankees' pinstripes has long been a source of pride for any ballplayer, even for those who began their careers elsewhere, often with the view that there was nothing better than beating the Yankees.

We offer behind-the-scenes shots of locker rooms past and present, where stirring speeches have preceded dynamic deeds on the diamond. But not everything changes: the locker of captain Thurman Munson, preserved since his untimely death in 1979, was moved to the museum in the Yankees' new stadium in 2009 and will forever commemorate a much-missed leader.

The New York Yankees are one of the world's legendary sports teams, and their story has never been less than fascinating. The unique "then and now" format of this book throws a new light on more than a century's worth of baseball history.

The Frieze p.72

Female Fans p.78

Stadium Scoreboard p.82

The Locker Room p.84

Remembering the Greats p.96

Historic Catches p.106

Celebrity Fans p.110

Yankee Fans Celebrate p.116

Yankee Stadium Aerial p.138

★ **The first recognized baseball league was** formed in 1858 at a convention in New York, with 22 attendant clubs agreeing on the formation of the National Association of Base Ball Players as well as forming a committee that would be charged with drafting a constitution and bylaws. Over the next four decades baseball would make significant strides, with regional leagues cropping up across the country.

One of these was the Western League, which had a fractured history, undergoing numerous reorganizations, until a more stable existence was established in 1893 with the appointment of Byron Bancroft "Ban" Johnson as president. He reorganized the league again at the end of the century, adding three teams from East Coast cities and renaming it the American League in a deliberate attempt to challenge the all-powerful

National League. Ban Johnson did not have things all his own way, however, for attempts to launch an American League club in New York were thwarted by the New York Giants, whose political influence was sufficient to prevent another club from setting up in the city. Instead, Johnson gave a franchise to Baltimore, a city that had been deserted by the National League in 1900. Nicknamed the Orioles and based at Oriole Park they were managed and part-owned by John McGraw, but problems would surface between Johnson and McGraw, resulting in McGraw leaving the Orioles for the New York Giants, although he frequently went back and signed Baltimore's best players.

Ban Johnson knew he had to orchestrate a truce between the Giants and the Orioles if the league was to survive. Key to his plan was to switch the Orioles from Baltimore to New York, which was put to a vote of National and American League clubs at a meeting in 1903. Only one club dissented, the New York Giants, thus enabling the Orioles to make the lucrative switch.

With new owners Frank J. Farrell and William S. Devery having paid $18,000 for the team and having found a suitable location for a ground that was not blocked by the Giants, the Orioles took up residence at their new ballpark, Hilltop Park. They were initially known as the New York Highlanders because of their elevated grounds and in reference to a British regiment known as the Gordon Highlanders—a play on the surname of team president Joseph Gordon. The credit for coining the Yankees moniker went to *New York Press* sports editor Jim Price, chiefly because "Yankees" fit newspaper headlines better than did "Americans," another of the team's nicknames.

As the decade passed, the Highlanders made steady progress. Although they did not win the American League, they did manage second-place finishes in 1904 and 1906, aided by key players such as Willie Keeler and Jack Chesbro, who first came to prominence in 1904 when his 41 wins set a single-season record that is unlikely to be topped. As the Highlanders reached the final stages of the season, there were hopes that they might be able to win the pennant, although the New York Giants announced, through John T. Brush, that they would not contest the World Series against the American League winners, sure that the Highlanders would prove to be the

winning team. However, the Giants' fears proved unfounded, for a final-game loss to the Boston Americans (now the Red Sox) dashed the Highlanders' hopes, with none other than Jack Chesbro being blamed for a wild pitch in the top of the ninth inning that allowed the winning run.

Fortunately, Willie Keeler continued to show consistency, and the Highlanders were to finish second again in 1906 and 1910, although not as close to the pennant as they had in 1904. At this time, the man who best exemplified the team was Clark Griffith. He would combine the roles of player and manager for the next four years, retiring as a player in 1907 in order to concentrate on management, but a falling-out with the club's owners in 1908 saw him fired midway through the season. Griffith would go on to make a name for himself as both a manager and owner—the New York Americans might well have been too hasty in disposing with his services in 1908.

LEFT: Nicknamed the "Old Fox," Clark Griffith played for the St. Louis Browns, Boston Reds, and Chicago Colts/Orphans before becoming player-manager for the Chicago White Stockings. Ban Johnson played a pivotal role in persuading Griffith to join the Highlanders in 1903, again taking up the post of player-manager.

FAR LEFT: Willie Keeler at bat against Boston in 1908. He would eventually leave in 1909, heading across town to join the Giants.

BELOW: The 1904 campaign proved to be the pinnacle of Jack Chesbro's career, as he suffered a drastic slump over the next few years.

GAME CHANGERS

KEY MOMENTS IN YANKEE HISTORY

THE HIGHLANDERS BECOME NEW YORK'S SECOND TEAM

ABOVE: Opening day of the 1908 season. Hilltop Park occupied one of the largest sites of the era. The seating capacity was around 16,000, with standing room for another 10,000.

The arrival of a second baseball franchise in New York was the result of peace breaking out between the two rival leagues in the United States. Major League Baseball is generally accepted as starting in April 1876 under the auspices of the National League. Various other leagues emerged as challengers, and in 1901 the American League declared itself a major league. Previous attempts by president Ban Johnson to place an American League team in New York City had been blocked, largely by the National League's New York Giants. As part of the negotiations with the league, Johnson was now able to get consent from all the National League's team owners, with only the Giants dissenting.

The Baltimore Orioles had been a struggling outfit, established in the American League in 1901 as Johnson's alternative to a New York franchise. In January 1903, the Orioles were purchased by gambling magnate Frank J. Farrell and police chief William S. Devery for $18,000 and moved to Manhattan. Two months later, the New York team was formally admitted to the American League. Devery took a back seat in management, and it was Farrell who funded the construction of the new ballpark at 168th Street and Broadway. Hilltop Park was situated to the north of Manhattan in the Washington Heights neighborhood, overlooking the Hudson River. The Giants' Polo Grounds was only a few blocks away to the southeast.

Construction of the all-wooden ballpark had to be started quickly, and was not fully completed for the opening home series of the 1903 season; the grandstand roof and some of the bleachers were missing. The clubhouse was not ready, either, forcing the players to change in a nearby hotel. The total cost was $275,000, largely because of the need to level out the terrain.

Officially called American League Park, the stadium quickly became known as Hilltop Park because of its location at one of the highest points in Manhattan. This in turn gave the team its

unofficial nickname, the Highlanders. William Randolph Hearst's paper the *New York Evening Chronicle* (which was pro-Giants) referred to the team mockingly as "the Invaders."

The opening day of Hilltop Park, April 30, 1903, saw a team put together by Ban Johnson beat the Washington Senators 6–2. Leading the team was pitcher-manager Clark Griffith, backed by a pitching staff that featured Jack Chesbro and left-hander Jesse Tannehill, both recruited from the National League's Pittsburgh Pirates. Also wearing the Yankees uniform that day were third baseman Wid Conroy and future Hall of Fame outfielder Willie Keeler, once a member of the Giants.

At the end of the season, the Highlanders finished respectably in fourth place in the eight-team league with a record of 76–62. Real success, however, was some years away.

ABOVE: The Highlanders, or the New York Americans as they were labeled in most early press photos, wait for the action to start on the opening day of the 1908 season at Hilltop Park.

BELOW: The crowd is a virtual sellout on opening day, April 16, 1908, at Hilltop Park. The Highlanders were playing the Philadelphia Athletics.

HILLTOP PARK

The wide-open spaces of Hilltop Park meant the Highlanders lost very few baseballs

LEFT: Hilltop Park, the original home of the New York Americans, hosts a game between the Chicago White Sox and the Highlanders in August 1909, with Rube Manning pitching. Just as the Highlanders were briefly known as the Greater New York Baseball Club, Hilltop Park was originally called American League Park; the words "American League" were displayed in large white letters by the main entrance. Its location at one of Manhattan's highest points led to it becoming known by the more familiar name of Hilltop Park. The stadium was built hastily over a six-week period prior to the 1903 season, and construction continued during the year. Hilltop had an unusually large field of play, as can be seen in this photo. The center-field fence initially stood at 542 feet, with right field at 400 feet, but an inner fence was soon constructed to encourage more offense.

BELOW: Batting practice at Hilltop Park on April 21, 1911, with the grandstand on the right. The Highlanders' landlord, the New York Institute for the Blind, was not inclined to renew the ten-year lease on the land, leaving the team searching for a new home. A proposed stadium on Kingsbridge Road, near the Harlem River Canal in the Bronx, proved abortive and the team went on to share the New York Giants' Polo Grounds for nine seasons beginning in 1913. The last major league game at Hilltop Park was played on October 5, 1912, when the Highlanders beat the Washington Senators 8–6. The ballpark was demolished in 1914.

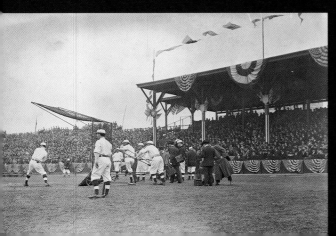

ABOVE: The New York Presbyterian Hospital now occupies the site of Hilltop Park in Washington Heights, seen here in 2012. After the ballpark was demolished in 1914, the land remained vacant until 1928, when construction of the hospital, originally called the Columbia Presbyterian Medical Center, began. It was opened later that year. The site contains a five-sided plaque to commemorate its history as a baseball field, placed there in 1993.

LEFT: Crowds lining up outside Hilltop Park were under no illusion as to which league they were watching.

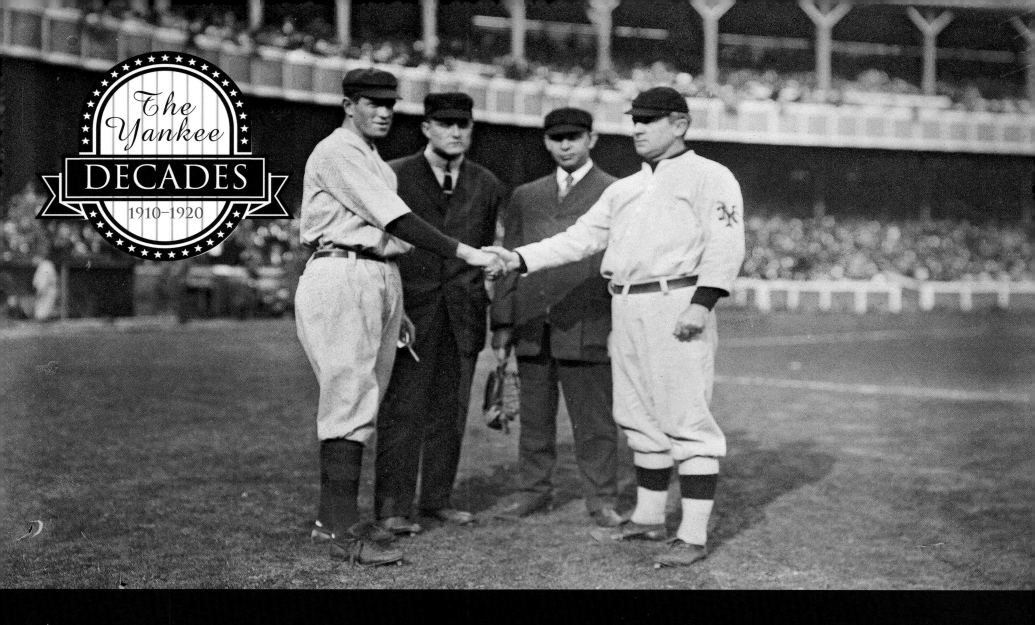

★ **Clark Griffith's sacking cost the Highlanders** dearly, both on and off the field. One of the key players he had brought to the club, Hal Chase, was adamant that he would not play for the new manager, Kid Elberfield. Of the 98 games played under Elberfield, only 27 were victories, giving him the worst winning percentage (.276) of any Yankees manager in history.

Fortunately, Hal Chase appeared to have a better impression of George Stallings, who took over in 1909 and managed the club for 295 games, of

which 152 were won, giving him a win percentage of .515. More importantly, he was able to steer the Highlanders back up the American League, guiding them to a second-place finish in 1910, the first time in four years they finished that high. Next to take the mantle was Hal Chase himself, whose 167 games resulted in 86 victories, enabling him to match Stallings's win percentage of .515—a remarkable achievement considering he was still playing on a regular basis. Chase stepped down as manager in 1911 but remained in the lineup for two more years, even signing a new three-year

contract in 1913. However, he was traded to the Chicago White Sox for Babe Borton and Rollie Zeider not long after the contract was signed.

There were other arrivals at Hilltop Park in 1911, with the New York Giants arriving en masse after a fire swept through their home park, the Polo Grounds, on April 14, 1911. The two clubs had endured an acrimonious start to their relationship, fueled by the Highlanders planting themselves in New York, but fortunately relations between the clubs had thawed significantly enough (even as McGraw was still manager of the Giants) for the Giants' owner, John T. Brush, to rent Hilltop Park from his rivals in a time of desperation. The gesture would be repaid in a few years.

The Highlanders, meanwhile, continued to search for consistency. After Clark Griffith's five-year tenure, the team had five managers in five years, every one falling short of the bar that had been set by Griffith. Matters were not helped by the increasingly perilous financial position of the team's owners and the sometimes surprising defeats the team suffered, some of which were sufficient to fuel rumors of fixed games, many revolving around Hal Chase.

Under such circumstances, the Highlanders were in need of a stimulus by 1913. They got it from the most unlikely of sources: when the Giants' home at the Polo Grounds was completely rebuilt, this time in concrete and steel in order to prevent any further mishaps from fire, the Highlanders were invited to make the journey to Manhattan to share the Giants' ballpark, officially known as Brush Stadium.

While Brush Stadium provided an almost constant reminder of their rivals' presence, there were other changes. The first of these concerned the team's name; since the ballpark was not elevated, it prompted a switch to the name by which they would become famous, the Yankees. The change was not unexpected.

By 1915 the partnership between the club's owners, Frank J. Farrell and William S. Devery, had deteriorated, with both in desperate need of funds. The only commodity either held with any real value was their ownership of the Yankees, prompting them to find a suitable buyer. They found two in brewing magnate Colonel Jacob Ruppert and Colonel Tillinghast L'Hommedieu Huston, who paid $460,000 for the franchise.

The Yankees now had the financial wherewithal to turn the team into a major player in baseball. The process would not happen overnight; the Yankees made slow progress up the American League, registering fourth-place finishes in 1916 and again in 1918. The following year they went one better, finishing third.

That third place came at a transitional time, not just for the Yankees but also for the world in general. After four years of fighting in Europe, World War I was at an end. Professional baseball continued through the war, although one player who did not return was former Yankees pitcher Alex Burr, who was killed in France on October 12, 1918.

FAR LEFT: Hal Chase (left) shakes the hand of the Giants' John McGraw before a game in 1910. Chase was often at the center of the allegations about fixing games, being accused twice by managers of the Highlanders for reportedly "laying down" during games. Chase would be charged in 1918, after his time with the Highlanders, but was acquitted due to a lack of evidence.

BELOW LEFT: The source of Ruppert's wealth, his brewery. The colonel paid $1.25 million to buy out his partner Huston in 1922, with confirmation of the $460,000 original purchase price appearing in several obituaries when Frank J. Farrell died in 1926.

BELOW: Alex Burr (seen here as a teenager in Choate, Illinois) was killed in 1918 when his plane collided with another over Cazaux in France, bursting into flames and plunging into a lake. Burr was one of eight major-league players killed during World War I.

GAME CHANGERS
KEY MOMENTS IN YANKEE HISTORY

THE FAMOUS PINSTRIPES FIRST APPEAR ON THE TEAM'S UNIFORMS

ABOVE: Bill Stumpf (pitching) shows off the new Highlanders' home uniforms at Hilltop Park in 1912.

The date was April 11, 1912. The Yankees were still known as the Highlanders and their home field was still the wooden structure at Hilltop Park. For the first game of the season, the Highlanders sported new uniforms with pinstripes. The first player to wear pinstripes in action was the hard-living 23-year-old Ray Caldwell, who threw the opening pitch of the season. The pinstripes design would eventually become synonymous with the Yankees, and became an essential part of the team's image and identity—making their home uniform one of the most famous and instantly recognizable in all sports.

Despite their automatic association with today's Yankees, the pinstripes were not an immediate success. In fact, they may even have been viewed as unlucky because, after the Highlanders lost 102 games in 1912, the pinstripes were abandoned for the next season, when the team changed its name to the Yankees. The pinstripes did not return until 1915, with a crucial modification. Originally the stripes were black, but the shade was altered to midnight blue, giving rise to the expression that the team's fans "bleed Yankee blue."

The spacing and size of the pinstripes has changed over the years. In Babe Ruth's heyday, the stripe was an eighth of an inch; now it is nearer to a tenth of an inch. The space between stripes has varied from 1 inch to 1.1 inches.

The Yankees made history again in 1929 when they became the first team to regularly put numbers on the back of their jerseys, a practice which the rest of Major League Baseball adopted by the mid-1930s. Initially, the numbers were allocated according to a player's place in the batting order.

However, the tradition-minded Yankees have not followed the rest of baseball by putting players' names on the backs of their jerseys.

ABOVE LEFT: George McConnell and Michael Cann in their pinstripes in front of a typical Hilltop Park backdrop in 1912. The Bronx Bombers were not the first baseball team to adopt pinstripes. The Chicago Cubs had used them on their road uniforms in 1907. Today, although several other major league clubs have pinstripes on some version of their uniforms, the Yankees will always be associated with the design.

.

ABOVE: Albert J. "Cozy" Dolan warming up at Hilltop Park in 1912. By the end of the season he would be traded to the Philadelphia Phillies.

POLO GROUNDS

A casualty of Yankee success

LEFT: An aerial shot of Yankee Stadium from the 1950s shows the proximity of the Polo Grounds across the Harlem River. After the Giants left for California at the end of the 1957 season, the Polo Grounds hosted the Mets for the 1962 and 1963 seasons. The bridge (top right) running from the 155th Avenue station crossed the Harlem River to Sedgwick Avenue in the Bronx. After the Ninth Avenue elevated railway ceased operation in 1940, the service across the river became known as the Polo Grounds Shuttle. It was discontinued in 1958, and the bridge was removed.

FAR RIGHT: The same view as it looked in 2006 after the extensive rebuilding of Yankee Stadium from 1973 to 1976, but before its demolition in 2010. The Polo Grounds was demolished in 1964 and a public housing project, the Polo Grounds Towers, stands in its place. The stadium wrecking crew tipped their hats to the old place by wearing Giants jerseys.

BELOW: The John T. Brush Stairway being rebuilt in September 2012. The stairway led down from Coogan's Bluff to the stadium. Brush owned the Giants from 1890 until his death in 1912.

GETTING TO THE POLO GROUNDS

Fans flock to the stadium for a game circa 1915. The original venue was built for polo in 1876, and the name stuck when the Giants relocated there. The Yankees were tenants from 1913 to 1922. The Giants finally moved out in 1957 when they left for San Francisco. The Polo Grounds were briefly occupied by the New York Mets from 1962 to 1963, and the ballpark was demolished in 1964. On the left, fans can be seen heading down what is now the John T. Brush Stairway.

THE HIGHLANDERS BECOME THE YANKEES

The perennially success-starved Yankees were not seen as a threat to the mighty New York Giants. Having loaned them Hilltop Park to allow the fire-stricken Polo Grounds to be rebuilt, the Giants returned the favor in 1913 after the Yankees' lease ran out on Hilltop Park. By the time the arrangement ended in 1923, things had changed considerably.

One effect of the move was that the nickname "Highlanders" was no longer appropriate. It was unpopular with sportswriters and editors because it couldn't be fitted into short newspaper columns. "New York Americans" wasn't much better. Newspapers had been referring to the team as the "Yanks" or "Yankees" as early as 1904, possibly before. The name derives from the British term for Americans, which was based on common names of early Dutch settlers in New York: *Janke*, or *Jan* and *Kee*. In baseball terms, it was often applied to teams playing in the American League, as opposed to the National League.

Another explanation is that around 1906, part of the crowd at Hilltop Park was fond of singing "Yankee Doodle Dandy" as the players came out onto the field, sometimes adapting the words to refer to "Yankee Doodle Griffith" in honor of manager-pitcher Clark Griffith. In any event, "Yankees" was already in common use in the media and among fans, and the club bowed to the inevitable by officially adopting it in the spring of 1913. Co-owners William S. Devery and Frank J. Farrell took the step largely as a marketing decision after consulting newspaper editors.

Other than the change of name, 1913 was another disappointing season for the Yankees; they finished next to last in the league with a 57–94 record. In contrast, the Giants pulled in 630,000 fans, tops in the National League.

LEFT: A floral tribute for manager Frank Chance at the opening game at the Polo Grounds in 1913. Chance had been dubbed the "Peerless Leader" by the Chicago press after he guided the Chicago Cubs to four National League pennants in five years between 1906 and 1910 and to World Series triumphs in 1907 and 1908. The Yankees' owners hoped he would work the same magic with their 1913 team. The word "Tammany" on the uniforms reveals the political background of co-owner Bill Devery. Chance, who also played in 12 games for the Yankees as a pinch hitter, failed to reproduce his successes and left after only two years to manage the Los Angeles Angels in the Pacific Coast League.

BELOW LEFT: Manager Frank Chance failed to get on with star player Hal Chase, who was traded in May for Babe Borton and Rollie Zeider in one of the worst trades in Yankees history. Zieder played just 50 games, and Borton had a batting average of .130.

BELOW: A rare moment: Babe Borton rounds the bases at the Polo Grounds in 1913.

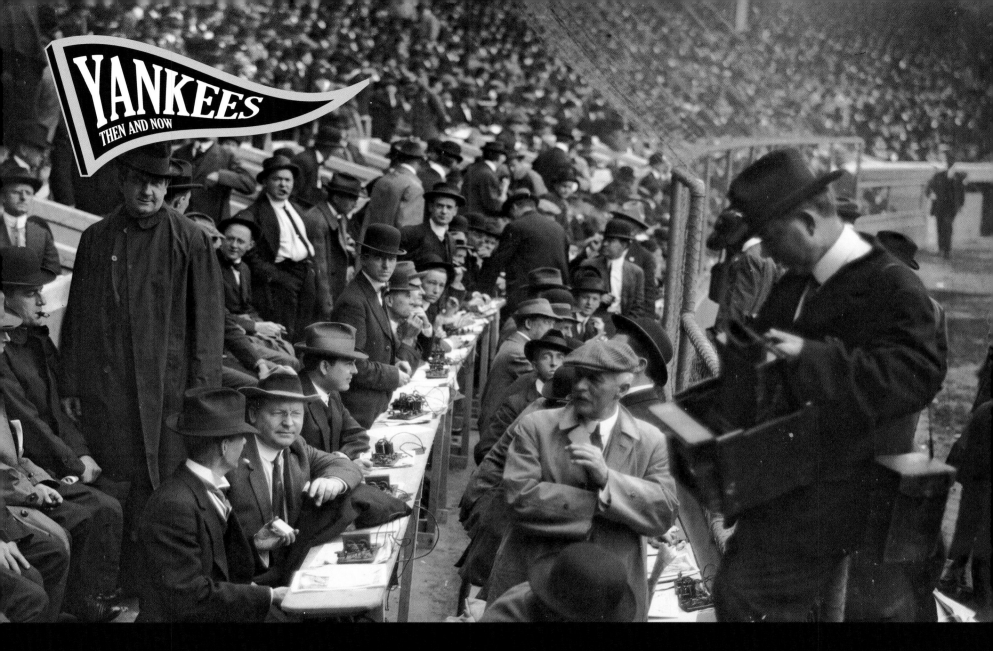

THE PRESS BOX

The Yankees have been big news for over a century

ABOVE: A view of the press box at the Polo Grounds circa 1915, with journalists and their telegraph machines poised to send reports on a Yankees game to newspapers around the nation. Radio would soon make these journalists' machines redundant.

RIGHT: NBC's Graham McNamee interviews Babe Ruth at Yankee Stadium during the 1923 World Series. A pioneering radio broadcaster, McNamee helped popularize play-by-play commentaries of games in the 1920s, and became one of the most recognizable voices on the airwaves at the time.

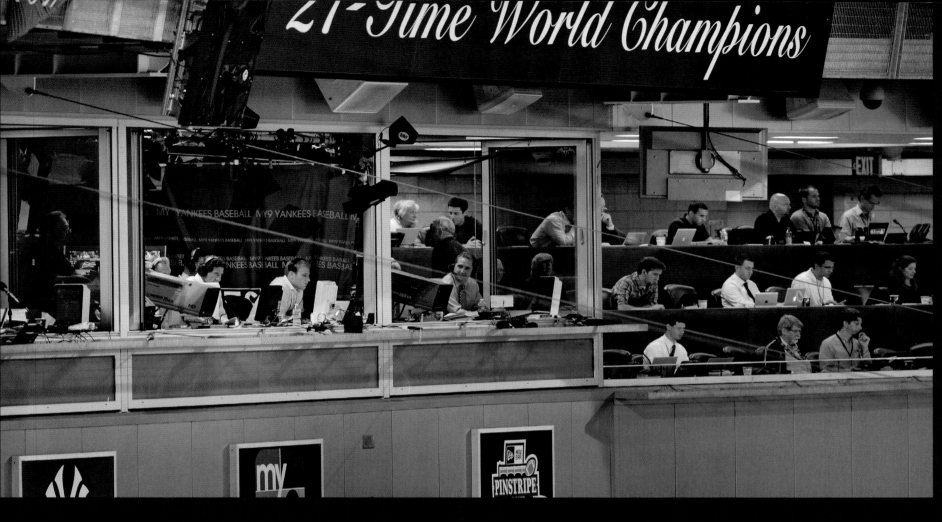

21-Time World Champions

ABOVE: Today's press box accommodates representatives from a global media, while the stadium's public-address announcer also operates from here. Games are televised on the YES Network and WWOR-TV, with radio coverage coming from WCBS (in English) and WADO (in Spanish).

RIGHT: Comedian Joe E. Brown (right) joins sportscaster Mel Allen in the press box during a game against the Boston Red Sox at Yankee Stadium in 1953. Brown was a promising baseball player who turned down the chance to join the Yankees in favor of a career in comedy. He combined the two enthusiasms in 1953 when he became a television and radio broadcaster. Allen began broadcasting Yankee games on the radio in 1939 and on television in the 1940s. He became synonymous with the team but was dismissed amid controversy in 1964.

GAME CHANGERS
KEY MOMENTS IN YANKEE HISTORY

BABE RUTH IS TRADED FROM THE BOSTON RED SOX

ABOVE: A subdued-looking "Bambino" in 1919, his final season with the Red Sox.

Babe Ruth made his debut for the Yankees' rivals, the Boston Red Sox, in July 1914, having been traded from the minor-league Baltimore Orioles a few months earlier. At this time, Ruth was primarily known for his skills as a pitcher. The Red Sox fielded an abundance of stars, which meant he only played five games for them in 1914. For the rest of the season, he was optioned to the minor-league Providence Greys who, with his help, won the International League pennant.

The Babe played for the Red Sox until 1919, appearing in three World Series, making a major pitching contribution in the 1915 and 1918 victories; in 1918 he set a World Series record by pitching 29 consecutive scoreless innings, a record that lasted until it was broken by Whitey Ford in 1961. The beginning of Babe Ruth's conversion to an outfielder also came in 1918, as he insisted on spending less time pitching and more in the batter's box. In the 1919 season, he established a new record for home runs with 29, a figure that he would surpass with the Yankees.

The world of baseball was shocked when the Red Sox sold Babe Ruth to New York in December 1919. Rumor had it that Boston's owner, theatrical impresario Harry Frazee, needed the money to finance a new Broadway musical, *No, No Nanette*. The reality is that Ruth was holding out for an increase in salary that would double his earnings. He threatened to quit baseball for supposedly more lucrative professions like boxing or acting. The Red Sox were heavily in debt and could not afford to agree to Ruth's financial demands.

Another factor forcing Frazee's hand was the player's reputation for misbehavior and drinking. In 1917 he had been suspended for 10 games for throwing a punch at an umpire during a game against the Washington Senators. The following year, he walked out on the team after a dispute with assistant manager Johnny Evers. There were concerns about Ruth's drinking habits before games as well.

Pressure applied by American League president Ban Johnson meant that Frazee was limited to trading with only the Chicago White Sox and the Yankees. Chicago offered a player-plus-cash deal that would have seen "Shoeless Joe" Jackson moving to Boston, but the offer from the cash-rich Yankees was more enticing. The $125,000 fee was more than double the previous highest trade in baseball history, and Yankees owners Ruppert and Huston also granted Frazee a $300,000 loan, with a mortgage on Fenway Park as collateral.

When the trade was announced in early January 1920, Frazee attempted to justify it by claiming that the Yankees were taking a big gamble with the player. In fact, the Yankees would establish a dynasty of success built around Ruth's power-hitting ability, something that would transform the sport of baseball itself. In his first season with the Yankees, Ruth completed his transition from pitcher to hitter, hitting 54 home runs and batting .376. His .847 slugging average was unsurpassed in the major leagues until 2001.

ABOVE: After the trade, the Red Sox would not win another World Series until 2004, and this "Curse of the Bambino" was put down to the trade, and was a key component in the Yankees–Red Sox rivalry. Furthermore, Ed Barrow, Boston's manager at the time, was recruited by the Yankees as business manager in 1920. He was a major influence on the Yankees' success over the next two decades.

BELOW: Owner Jacob Ruppert and Babe Ruth discuss his disciplinary fine in 1925.

★ **The New York Yankees had made two major** acquisitions toward the end of the 1910s: Miller Huggins was hired as manager in 1918, and a year later a player named Babe Ruth arrived. Huggins had been recommended to the Yankees by Ban Johnson, but Ruppert, who interviewed him, was not entirely impressed. Huston was in Europe at the time the appointment was made and was known to be strongly opposed, favoring another

choice. The appointment of Huggins drove a wedge between Ruppert and Huston that culminated in the partners falling out and Ruppert buying out Huston's share of the club in 1922.

Although small in stature, Miller Huggins was mentally strong and imposed his will on the team right from the start. This meant many hours of practice, going over each and every aspect of the

game. The endless practicing infuriated several players—none more so than Babe Ruth, who felt the spontaneous nature of baseball meant that it was almost impossible to practice or prepare for something you didn't expect. Although the initial relationship between the manager and star player was fractious, eventually the manager won, but not without having to fine or suspend Ruth whenever he felt he was out of line.

After finishing third in 1919, the Yankees started the new decade with the same result, but the following season won their very first league pennant. It was not only on the field that the Yankees were making great strides, for their popularity, aided almost totally by the presence of Babe Ruth, resulted in them drawing bigger crowds to the Polo Grounds than their landlords, the Giants. As the two teams prepared to battle it out in the 1921 World Series, John T. Brush served notice on the Yankees to leave the Polo Grounds. Giants manager John McGraw rubbed salt in the wound by stating that the Yankees should "move to some out-of-the-way place, like Queens."

Ruppert and Huston searched extensively for a plot of land sufficient to accommodate their grand plans for a stadium, and eventually settled for a lumberyard in the Bronx, close enough to the Polo Grounds to ensure that the Yankees would remain a thorn in the side of the Giants for many years to come. After the partners paid $600,000 for the land, a magnificent ballpark that could hold up to 58,000 fans was constructed in less than a year at a cost of $2.4 million ($32 million today). That the capacity was nearly double that of other baseball parks was indicative of how popular the Yankees had become, and while officially it was called Yankee Stadium, it earned the unofficial name of "the House that Ruth Built."

Gradually, the combination of stable ownership, an expert manager, and top players like Babe Ruth began to make an impact. The Yankees may have lost their first two World Series, both against the Giants, but on and off the field they were beginning to pull away from their rivals. More important, they were putting considerable distance between themselves and just about everyone else in their league. A third consecutive pennant was won in 1923, earning the team another chance at the Giants and the World Series. The third time proved to be the charm, as the Yankees registered a 4–2 victory that would ultimately see Babe Ruth named Most Valuable Player. No wonder the "sold out" signs were going up at Yankee Stadium on a regular basis.

FAR RIGHT: Two thirds of the legendary "Murderers' Row" (from left to right): Earl Combs, Bob Meusel, Lou Gehrig, and Babe Ruth.

BELOW RIGHT: At the beginning of the 1920s, Babe Ruth made extra money in the off-season selling hand-rolled cigars. By the end of the decade, he was an international sports star.

BELOW: Babe Ruth rolling over Lou Archer in the silent comedy *Babe Comes Home* (1927). Ruth had a short-lived Hollywood career. Both this film and *Speedy*, with Harold Lloyd, were directed by Ted Wilde.

As is often the case, having reached the pinnacle of success, the Yankees suffered a dip in form over the next couple of years. A second-place finish in the American League in 1924 was followed by a virtual collapse a year later when the Yankees finished in seventh place. That season had seen the biggest threat to Miller Huggins's authority, with Babe Ruth suspended for "misconduct on the playing field" and also hit with a $5,000 fine. Ruth was so certain in his value to the team that he expected Jacob Ruppert to rescind the fine, stating that he would never play for Huggins again. Ruppert announced that not only did he have faith in the manager, whom he expected to remain as manager, but that he would back each and every decision. Ruth was the one who backed down, apologizing to the manager and owner and paying his fine. It proved to be the turning point to propel the Yankees back to the top.

The American League pennant returned to New York in 1926, although the St. Louis Cardinals won the World Series in seven games. While the main story of the 1927 season was Babe Ruth's home-run record of 60, there were other reasons to celebrate. After registering a 110–44 record in

the regular season (the best since the Chicago Cubs in 1906) and capturing the pennant by 19 games, the Yankees were big favorites to win the World Series.

Their 4–0 World Series victory over the Pittsburgh Pirates was impressive, but the form of some of the new guns on the team, most notably Lou Gehrig, who was named Most Valuable Player, bode well for the future. Indeed, so potent a force were the Yankees that the first six hitters—Earle Combs, Mark Koenig, Babe Ruth, Lou Gehrig, Bob Meusel, and Tony Lazzeri—were known as "Murderers' Row." (The nickname had originally been bestowed on the Yankees' 1918 lineup, but the phrase is more often associated with the all-conquering 1927 team.)

Another notable name was Waite Hoyt, the mainstay of the Yankees' six championships in the 1920s. Nicknamed "Schoolboy," the fresh-faced pitcher enjoyed a 21-year career, leaving the

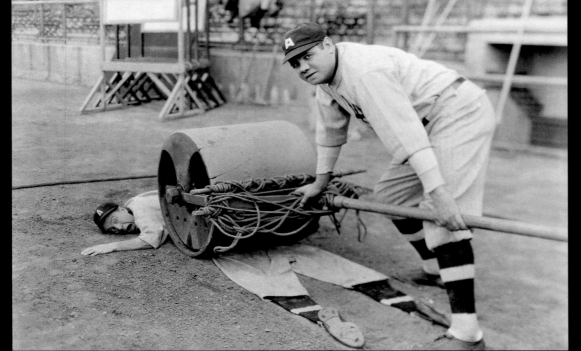

Yankees in 1930 for a new job in broadcasting. He was elected to the National Baseball Hall of Fame in 1969.

The American League title was retained the following season as the Yankees fought off a growing threat from the Philadelphia Athletics before sweeping the St. Louis Cardinals in the World Series. With minimal changes to the team, the Yankees were confident that their run of success would continue into the 1929 season, but the up-and-coming Athletics proved to have the

ascendancy, and the Yankees finished second in the American League.

Almost as soon as the realization set in that the league had passed the Yankees by, Miller Huggins began consulting with the coaches as to what changes would be necessary for the coming season. He wanted the pennant back and was prepared to make bold decisions on the team. Unfortunately, whatever plans he had worked on were never brought to fruition, for in September 1929 he was admitted to a hospital, initially being

diagnosed with erysipelas, although he also developed influenza. He died on September 25, five days after being admitted; the American League canceled all games the following day out of respect. Huggins's death dealt the Yankees a huge blow, as the loss of the most successful manager in the team's history created a void that took considerable time to fill. During Miller's 11-year tenure, the Yankees won the American League pennant on six occasions and the World Series three times, effectively creating a benchmark for future Yankees managers.

Babe Ruth

Babe Ruth requires no introduction to baseball fans. He is credited by many as the man who changed the game. His heavy-hitting style altered the way baseball was played on the field, while his popularity and celebrity changed the way the public viewed what is now considered America's favorite pastime. Ruth set countless major league records during his 21-year professional career, and while some were inevitably surpassed, many still stand today. He is, quite simply, one of the greatest baseball players of all time—an American icon.

But things didn't come easy for the Babe, born George Herman Ruth Jr. in February 1895. He grew up in Baltimore, Maryland, to George Sr. and Kate. Out of eight children just he and his sister, Mamie, survived infancy; his childhood was no walk in the park. Ruth, with typical understatement, described it as "rough." Recognizing the potential to head down the wrong path, his parents sent him to a local Catholic boarding school to give him the stability and discipline that they were unable to provide due to their long hours at their jobs. These 12 years at boarding school would change Ruth's life, as it was there that he was introduced to baseball.

His natural talent discovered, it wasn't long before Ruth was snapped up professionally. He began his career with a minor league team, the Baltimore Orioles, as a 19-year-old, in 1914, though Ruth's age meant that club owner Jack Dunn had to sign as his legal guardian to complete the move. It was no big deal for Dunn, who knew that Ruth was a fine pitcher and hitter, but the unlikely arrangement gave birth to the name that would follow Ruth throughout his career. His Orioles teammates joked that he was Jack's newest babe—and the name stuck.

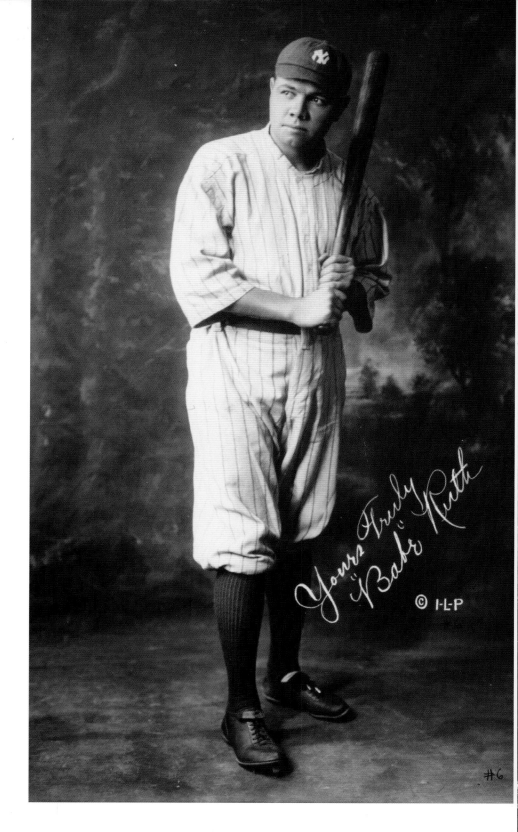

Yours Truly "Babe Ruth"

© I·L·P

#6

The man known for the sheer power with which he hit a baseball actually started out as a pitcher. However, his stint with the Orioles lasted less than half a year, and he was soon traded to the Boston Red Sox. Ruth's all-around prowess saw him record pitching statistics that were among the best in the league, but during his few times at bat it was quickly becoming clear where his true talent lay. In Boston he began his transformation to a full-time hitter, but not before he helped the Red Sox to their fifth World Series in 1918—as a pitcher.

Things were going well for Ruth both personally and professionally. He was already making quite the name for himself in the game, and in 1914 he married his fiancée, waitress Helen Woodford. Five years later, and a year after the Red Sox' World Series victory, Ruth was sold to the New York Yankees. It would be a relationship that

ABOVE RIGHT: Such was the Babe's fame and baseball's ascendency in the 1920s that Ruth started picking up film roles, this one with comedian Harold Lloyd in *Speedy* (1928).

BELOW: Yet another moment of high drama from his career, Babe Ruth is knocked unconscious after running into a concrete wall at Griffith Stadium in Washington, D.C., while trying to catch a foul ball on July 5, 1924.

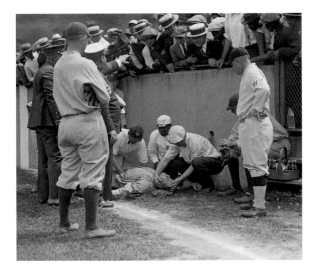

defined both the player and the club for the next decade and a half.

Ruth hit the ground running with the Yankees upon his arrival in 1920. Now a full-time batter and right fielder, his hard-hitting style meant that home runs were no longer a rare occurrence, and put offense at the top of the agenda. Ruth is credited with changing the very way baseball is played. Once a more tactical affair where games were won and lost with fairly low scores, Ruth's slugging kick-started a much more attacking philosophy—and scoring rocketed as a result.

In his first season, Ruth hit a record 54 home runs, more than double any of his rivals, helping the Yankees to their first American League pennant. But it was the following year that saw him etch his name into the history books, beating his home run record by five and smashing a host of other stats—including a slugging percentage of .846, something never seen before—and helping the Yankees retain their pennant and appear in their first World Series.

It's no coincidence that Ruth's arrival at the Polo Grounds, and subsequently Yankee Stadium, chimed with the accolades flooding in for the Yankees. Ruth helped them to their first-ever World Series win against the Giants in 1923, in which he hit three homers and was walked no less than eight times. Ruth would help the Yankees secure three more World Series titles, the second coming in 1927 against the Pittsburgh Pirates. This was another banner year that saw the Babe smash his own single-season home-run record for a third time, this time hitting 60 as part of the dominant Yankees lineup known as "Murderers' Row."

Babe Ruth's first wife, Helen, died in 1929, leaving him a daughter, Dorothy. But he soldiered on, both personally and professionally, winning his fourth and final World Series in 1932. The series against the Chicago Cubs may always be known

for Ruth's "called shot." The moment is shrouded in legend, largely due to differing accounts of the incident, but it is claimed that in game three of the series, Ruth predicted to the Cubs' pitcher and fielders that on the next ball he would smash a home run. Sure enough, he hit it—his second of the game and the last World Series home run of his career.

The Babe departed the Yankees in 1934, fully intent on retiring but staying in the game as a manager. That desire took him to the Northern League's Boston Braves in 1935 as a player at the age of 40, though with the promise of a future career as a manager. It never happened, and Ruth retired from the game for good after just one season with the team. He finished with a career total of 714 home runs.

A year later he was inducted into the newly formed Baseball Hall of Fame as one of its first five inductees, a hint of the many honors to come for a man many considered the best. Ruth died of cancer in 1948 at the age of 53; his number 3 was retired by the Yankees as the ultimate mark of respect. His effect on the game is still seen everywhere, from awards named in his honor right down to the records in the history books.

THE YANKEES WIN THEIR FIRST AMERICAN LEAGUE PENNANT

ABOVE: The sixth game of the World Series at the Polo Grounds on October 11, 1921. The Yankees are watching the Giants practice.

The year of 1921 was a crucial one for baseball. The sport was in transition from a tactical, slow-paced game to a faster, more spectacular affair, as exemplified by the slugging style of Babe Ruth. Baseball was also coming to terms with two of the darkest episodes in its history, the 1919 "Black Sox" game-fixing scandal and the death of Cleveland shortstop Ray Chapman, hit in the head by a pitch from the Yankees' Carl Mays at the Polo Grounds in August 1920.

The Indians recovered from the tragedy to take the American League pennant after an exciting three-way race with the Yankees and the Red Sox. The Yankees were striving to bury their old image of being an unlucky, losing team. Since being purchased by Ruppert and Huston in 1915, the club possessed financial clout, yet the pennant remained elusive.

The owners replaced manager "Wild" Bill Donovan with Miller Huggins in 1918. A small, introspective man, Miller was unpopular with many fans and journalists, and had difficulties dealing with big, boisterous players like Babe Ruth, who resisted his attempts at discipline. Nevertheless, his knowledge of baseball was unrivaled and he set about assembling a championship-caliber team. There was a steady if unspectacular improvement, with fourth place secured in 1918 and third in 1919, though midseason slumps following bright starts cost them the title both years.

In the off-season, the Bronx Bombers had appointed former Boston manager Ed Barrow as the club's new general manager. A major part of Barrow's role was to sign players, and he soon completed an eight-player trade with the Red Sox; incoming players included catcher Wally Schang and pitcher Waite Hoyt. Expectations for the 1921 season were growing. Babe Ruth was in his second year with the Yankees, having shattered the single-season home-run record in his first. Huggins was building his team's offense around the Babe. The season began with an 11–1

trouncing of Philadelphia Athletics at the Polo Grounds on April 13. The Indians remained the biggest threat to the Yankees' bid for the title.

In addition to Ruth, who turned in possibly the greatest single-season performance of all time, the 1921 Yankees boasted a powerful offensive roster. Schang knocked in 77 runs, and batted .316, with a .428 on-base percentage. Wally Pipp drove in 97 runs, scored 96 runs, and batted .296. Second baseman Aaron Ward batted .306, drove in 75 runs, and scored 77 runs. Roger Peckinpaugh had his best season, with 128 runs and batting .288, with a .380 on-base percentage. Outfielder Bob Meusel contributed 24 home runs and 135 RBIs, while also scoring 104 runs and batting .318.

The pitching staff was equally strong. Carl Mays led the league with a record of 27–9 and 337 innings pitched, and threw 30 complete games while compiling a 3.05 ERA. Waite Hoyt won 19 games, compiled an ERA of 3.09, and threw 21 complete games. Bob Shawkey contributed 18 victories and 18 complete games.

The Yankees won their first-ever American League pennant by 4½ games over the Indians to set up the first all–New York World Series with the Giants. The Yankees were favorites to win the so-called Subway Series. The rivalry between the two teams was intense. Giants manager John McGraw resented the increasing popularity of the upstart Yankees, and he was scathing about his rivals' power-hitting approach, believing baseball to be a scientific sport, built around single runs.

In their first World Series appearance, the Yankees won the opening two games, both by 3–0. The Giants rallied, seizing five out of the next six games in the best-of-nine series, clinching the world title on October 13, winning 1–0 in the eighth game. Babe Ruth's effectiveness was limited by injuries to his knee and in particular a laceration to his arm sustained in game three. Victory was sweet for McGraw and the Giants— but the Yankees would be back.

ABOVE: Babe Ruth wears the crown given to him by fans in 1921, honoring him as the "Sultan of Swat."

BELOW: A photo from the first game at the Polo Grounds in the 1921 season. Babe Ruth poses with teammate John "Home Run" Baker. A crowd of 40,000 turned out to see the Babe collect five hits.

YANKEES

THEN AND NOW

MANCUSO BROS
M'F'RS
REPAIRING
CURLING
CLEANING
DYEING
2602 8'AV. COR. 139 ST.

ONCE UPON A TIME IN THE BRONX

The site destined to become Yankee Stadium didn't look like prime real estate, but it soon became hallowed ground

LEFT: When the Yankees began their tenancy of the New York Giants' Polo Grounds in 1913, their landlords did not perceive the struggling team as a threat—but the ambitious Yankees soon developed into a force to be reckoned with. The acquisition of Babe Ruth prior to the 1920 season saw them pull in bigger crowds than the Giants, who asked them to leave, hoping that they would relocate to a distant corner of New York. This occasioned a citywide search for a suitable piece of land to house a new stadium. Sites in Queens and Upper Manhattan were considered before the Yankees' owners decided on a dilapidated 10-acre lumberyard in the Bronx, less than a mile from the Polo Grounds. The stadium was designed by Osborne Engineering, and construction was completed in just 284 days. The land, pictured here in 1921, was purchased from the wealthy William Waldorf Astor.

ABOVE: The original Yankee Stadium witnessed 26 World Series triumphs and underwent extensive renovations in the mid-1970s. In 2005 plans were announced to build a brand-new ballpark across the street from the original, which was to be demolished and the land converted into a public facility named Heritage Park. Its baseball and softball fields, which use the same turf as Yankee Stadium, are visible in this view from the original E-line subway stop at 161st Street.

ABOVE: A panoramic view of Heritage Park seen in September 2012. The costs of constructing the new stadium spiraled from the original estimate of $50.8 million to $195.6 million. Heritage Park was a replacement for the public land on which the new Yankee Stadium was built. Much of the park commemorates the history of the Yankees and the original stadium. The old diamond and outfield have been preserved, marked out by five-foot-wide swaths of blue polymer fiber stitched into the earth, while a 12-ton section of the iconic Yankee Stadium frieze is located in the northeast corner (seen here in the center of the photo).

THE HOUSE THAT WHITE BUILT

White Construction created a ballpark that would last for fifty years

ABOVE: Construction of the Yankees' new ballpark began on May 5, 1922, the day after a press conference at which the White Construction Company, chosen from more than forty bidders, signed the contract for the project. The company estimated that 2,000 tons of steel and 18,000 cubic

yards of reinforced concrete would be required to build the stadium. It was evident that this was to be the biggest sports arena in the United States. Plans for a three-tier stadium with a capacity of 85,000 were scaled down to a still-impressive venue with 58,000 seats. At the start of the project,

no name had been selected, but co-owner Jacob Ruppert commented that it would probably be called Yankee Field. Ultimately, the size and scale of the ballpark meant that it attracted the grander title of "Stadium." Work began without ceremony and was completed by February 1923.

ABOVE: A 1923 view along the third-base side of the completed grandstand showing the upper deck and the frieze in place.

BELOW: The completed stadium in 1923.

ABOVE: Today the site has been cleared and turned into a public space, but with the new stadium next door rather than built over the old, it is still possible to trace the historic footprint of "the House that Ruth Built." A giant Louisville Slugger baseball bat, in the style favored by Babe Ruth—and complete with frayed tape on the handle for extra authenticity—was installed outside when the stadium was extensively remodeled between 1973 and 1976. The 138-foot-tall bat was used to disguise an exhaust outlet, but standing just out front, it rapidly became a meeting spot where fans met up with their friends, prompting the message "Meet you at the bat."

YANKEE STADIUM OPENS

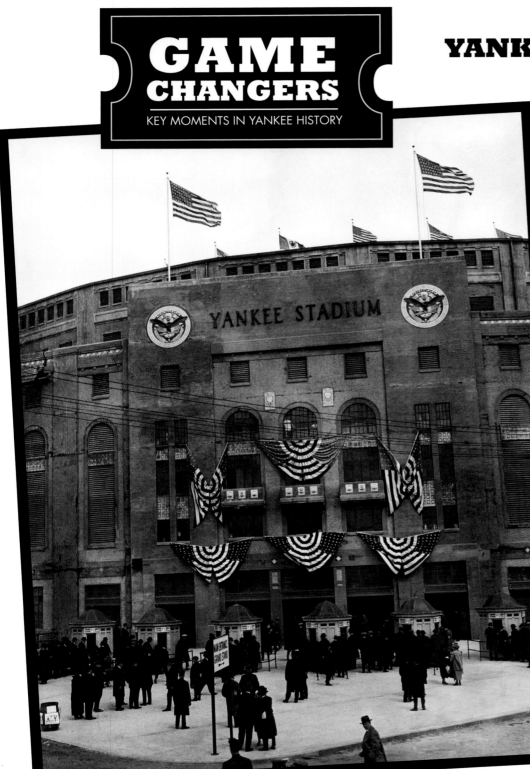

Since 1913, the Yankees had been tenants of the New York Giants at the Polo Grounds in the upper part of Manhattan. Relations between the two clubs were strained and got worse after Babe Ruth joined the Yankees in 1920. His box-office appeal soon saw the Yankees pulling in bigger crowds than their landlords. Despite the Giants' victory in the 1921 World Series, owner Charles Stoneham gave the Yankees notice to leave the Polo Grounds.

Brewing magnate Colonel Jacob Ruppert and his business partner Colonel Tillinghast L'Hommedieu Huston had purchased the Yankees from Frank J. Farrell and William S. Devery in 1915. The construction of a new stadium represented a major risk for them, particularly as they gambled on a building with a capacity of 60,000, twice the size of most baseball facilities at that time. Their trump card was Babe Ruth. The owners were confident that Ruth would continue to draw in fans in large numbers. However, baseball had been tainted and its popularity diminished by the 1919 Black Sox scandal when eight Chicago White Sox players were found guilty of fixing games in the World Series, adding a further undercurrent of uncertainty to the venture.

The Yankees scoured New York City for a suitable site, and eventually paid $600,000 for a 10-acre lumberyard in the west Bronx, just across the Harlem River from the Polo Grounds. Construction began in May 1922 and the stadium opened just under a year later on April 18, 1923. The pregame festivities included composer John Philip Sousa leading the New York's Seventh Regiment Band through "The Star Spangled Banner" and state governor Al Smith throwing the ceremonial first pitch. The official capacity of the stadium was 58,000, and there was a full house for opening day, although a somewhat exaggerated figure of 74,217 was subsequently claimed. Either way, it was a record attendance for baseball.

LEFT: Opening day at Yankee Stadium, 1923. The Yankees drew just over one million in the first season, but attendances were flat in the 1920s.

The Yankees' opponents were Ruth's former team, the Boston Red Sox, and the game ended in a 4–1 victory for the home side. Ruth hit a three-run homer into the right-field stands, the first in the new stadium that was soon dubbed "the House that Ruth Built" by Fred Lieb, a sportswriter for the *New York Evening Telegram*.

The original dimensions of the stadium were designed to capitalize on Ruth's hitting prowess. The field of play was unusually large. Its short right-field fence favored the Babe's left-handed power. For right-handed hitters, its deep left and center fields made home runs difficult. These areas became known as "Death Valley" after many batters watched towering fly balls die there.

The word "stadium" was applied to a baseball venue for the first time, reflecting the scale and ambition of the new facility. For the first time in North America, a three-tier design was used. This was initially limited to the left- and right-field corners, but was extended before the 1927 season.

Perhaps the most distinctive aspect of Yankee Stadium was its frieze. Gently curling around the upper deck of the grandstand, the copper latticework structure soon became an enduring symbol of both the stadium and the team. It was painted white in the 1960s. Unusually for a ballpark, it was decorative rather than functional, and cast a distinctive shadow across the field in the afternoon sun. The American flag in the field of play was another notable aspect. Flags were also flown outside the stadium, traditionally the Stars and Stripes alongside the New York City and New York State flags.

Yankee Stadium would be the scene of some of baseball's greatest moments and would host more World Series games than any other. The historic venue would go on to host football, soccer, and thirty championship boxing bouts, including Muhammad Ali against Ken Norton in 1976. Three papal masses were said at the stadium. It's no wonder the stadium was known as "the Cathedral of Baseball."

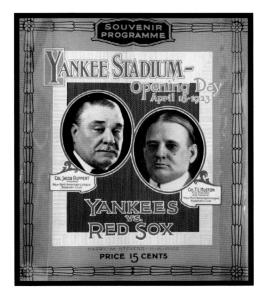

ABOVE: The opening-day program for Yankee Stadium featuring the two colonels, Ruppert and Huston, on the cover.

BELOW LEFT: The architect's plans for the new stadium as released in 1921. The new 75,000-seat stadium was described as being "the country's first ballpark."

BELOW: Babe Ruth (left) leads the Yankees onto the field on opening day.

YANKEE STADIUM: OPENING DAY

Ruppert had built a cathedral to baseball, and the congregation was not slow to arrive

ABOVE: Opening day of the original Yankee Stadium was April 18, 1923, when the inaugural fixture saw the Bronx Bombers face their fiercest rivals, the Boston Red Sox. The venue was packed to the rafters with a record crowd, and thousands of disappointed fans were left milling around

outside when the fire department finally closed the gates; more than 25,000 people were turned away. Governors, generals, politicians, and league officials were in attendance for the dedication ceremonies. John Philip Sousa and the U.S. Army Seventh Regiment Band led the teams to the

flagpole in center field, where the American flag and the Yankees' 1922 American League pennant were hoisted. The Yankees won 4–1 with Babe Ruth christening the new stadium with a three-run homer into the right-field seats.

ABOVE AND LEFT: The 1976 "Big Bat" is the most obvious reminder of the old Yankee Stadium site. It now stands outside the Metro North Station, built in 2009. A 450-foot-long pedestrian walkway and its staircase meet here. In the photo on the left, the new Yankee Stadium is visible in the background. It was opened with considerable fanfare on April 16, 2009. The season was ten days old and the Yankees had spent that time on the road in Baltimore, Kansas City, and Tampa Bay. It was a sunny spring day in the Bronx as fans entered the new stadium with the bittersweet sight of the original, soon to be demolished, just across the street. Some fans would have seen the workout day held two weeks previously and the exhibition games against the Chicago Cubs, but this was real thing, the new venue's first regular-season game.

NEW HOME RUN RECORD FOR BABE RUTH

ABOVE: Babe Ruth practices before the World Series in Philadelphia on October 5, 1927.

During the 1927 season, much attention was focused on the Yankee hitters whose prowess earned the team the nickname of "Murderer's Row." Along with Babe Ruth and Lou Gehrig, the Yankees' offense boasted Earle Combs, Mark Koenig, Bob Meusel, and Tony Lazzeri. The pitchers, who led the league in ERA at 3.20, also played a major role in creating a new record total of wins as the Yankees finished the regular season with 110 wins. The previous mark of 105 was set by the Boston Red Sox in 1905, and the Yankees' total would remain the best until it was surpassed by the Cleveland Indians in 1954. The Bronx Bombers led the American League from start to finish, ending up 19 games ahead of the second-place Philadelphia A's, who were led by Ty Cobb.

The American public was distracted from a minor game-fixing scandal, involving Detroit and Cleveland, by the slugging exploits of Babe Ruth and Lou Gehrig. Fans were enthralled by Ruth's attempt to better his own record of 59 home runs. For a time, it seemed that Gehrig might beat him to the task. He kept pace with Ruth, nudging ahead in midseason, until September, when both men were tied at 45. During that month, Ruth slugged a remarkable 17 homers to bring himself within reach of the target. The record-breaking 60th came on September 30, the next-to-last day of the season. Ruth faced Tom Zachary of the Washington Senators at Yankee Stadium, prompting unprecedented scenes of jubilation when he hit the famous homer off Zachary's third pitch. Gehrig finished the season with 47 homers. Between them, the two accounted for almost 25 percent of the home runs in the American League.

More records tumbled in 1927. Ruth slugged .772, batted .356, and drove in 164 runs. Gehrig's slugging percentage was .765; he batted .308 and drove in 149 runs. Third in runs scored was leadoff man Earle Combs with 137. Overall, the 1927 Yankees batted .307, slugged .489 (the best ever), scored 975 runs (another record), and outscored their opponents by a remarkable 376 runs. Pitchers Wiley Moore, Waite Hoyt, and Urban

Shocker were first, second, and fourth in ERA at 2.28, 2.64, and 2.84. Four Yankees pitchers exceeded .700 in win percentage. The pitching staff also led the American League in shutouts, as well as the fewest hits and walks allowed.

The Yankees swept the Pittsburgh Pirates in the World Series, the first time that an American League team had swept a National League team in the World Series. The Yankees' pitchers allowed only six extra-base hits in the series. Babe Ruth hit the only two home runs of the series. Shortstop Mark Koenig, who scored 99 runs in the regular season, had 9 hits in 18 at bats. Six future Hall of Famers were featured on the 1927 roster: Babe Ruth, Lou Gehrig, Herb Pennock, Waite Hoyt, Tony Lazzeri, and Earle Combs. Manager Miller Huggins was also inducted into the Hall of Fame. Little wonder that the Yankees of 1927 are still venerated by many as the greatest team ever in the history of the game.

ABOVE: The headline that would not be rewritten for 34 years.

BELOW: Members of the 1927 Yankees who had appeared in five World Series: Waite Hoyt, Babe Ruth, Miller Huggins, Bob Meusel, and Bob Shawkey.

ABOVE: Mickey Mantle signs a baseball for a tongue-tied young fan in the early 1950s.

LEFT: In April 1932, Babe Ruth autographs a baseball for heavyweight boxing champion Max Schmeling at League Park in Cleveland.

BELOW: A baseball signed by Babe Ruth is on display at an auction at Butterfields in Los Angeles in November 2001.

1932

SIGNING BASEBALLS
Ruth and Mantle memorabilia have always been in high demand

BELOW LEFT: A baseball signed by Babe Ruth was on display during an auction preview on November 2, 2001, at Butterfields in Los Angeles. The sale price of such items depends on the condition of the ball and the authentication of the signature. Most sought after by collectors are autographed official American League balls, made by Reach or Spalding, with red and blue stitching and little wear and tear. Ruth's signature is one of the most highly prized in the sport and, like most things connected with the Babe, the bolder the better. Quotation marks around the name "Babe" can add to the value, as these indicate that the signature was pre-1928. The finest known Ruth-autographed ball was sold privately for $150,000 in 2005. Of more recent signed artifacts, Mickey Mantle's 1952 Topps baseball card is one of the most expensive and sought-after baseball cards in the world. Depending on the condition and grading of the card, it can sell for over $25,000. A signed Mantle ball can be in the $400 to $1,000 range depending on the clarity of the signature, where the signature is located on the baseball (sweet spot), and the condition of the ball. The rise in popularity of sports memorabilia and limited-edition signed items helped Mickey Mantle generate income in his later years after many of his business investments (such as the Mickey Mantle Country Cookin' restaurant chain) foundered. He was the top draw at any baseball card show and could charge accordingly. Typical of the player that he was, it is said that he often insisted the promoters invite one of his lesser-known Yankee teammates to help them generate cash as well.

ABOVE: Derek Jeter signs autographs after a workout at the Yankees' spring-training complex at Legends Field in Tampa, Florida, in 2007.

RIGHT: A detail from a larger display of baseballs autographed by Yankee players past and present in the museum at Yankee Stadium.

★ **It took the New York Yankees three years** to find a more-than-adequate replacement for Miller Huggins, but the man who eventually stepped into the void would prove to be every bit as masterful. After cutting his managerial teeth with Louisville in 1919, Joe McCarthy had made his reputation with the Chicago Cubs, guiding them to the National League title in 1929, but he was sacked toward the end of the 1930 season. That decision proved to be of benefit to the

Yankees, for they hired him in 1931 as they looked to end a three-year title drought.

The appointment of McCarthy was another that was not universally popular, with Babe Ruth known to have designs on becoming manager himself and resenting McCarthy for being an outsider. Others would claim that McCarthy was fortunate that he inherited a talented squad and had little to do with their eventual success. Joe

McCarthy was strict but fair, a disciplinarian who kept the players in line but also allowed them a certain degree of autonomy. It was a style that would elevate the New York Yankees to the very pinnacle of the game, achieving unrivaled success that made them the premier team across the major leagues. It helped to have the likes of Babe Ruth on the team, but McCarthy did not allow the star to step out of line, a move that proved to be of major benefit to both Ruth and the entire team.

At the top of the American League in 1932 after a three-year absence, the Yankees swept the Chicago Cubs in the World Series, stretching the team's streak of consecutive games won in the World Series to 12, establishing a record that would last for the rest of the century. As a former manager of the Cubs, the result was especially pleasing for McCarthy, but he was never one to rest on his laurels.

McCarthy's intention that this would be just the start of a virtual domination of the game would take a while to accomplish. Despite Ruth hitting his 700th home run in 1934 (his last season with the Yankees) and the acquisition of Joe DiMaggio from the San Francisco Seals (for $25,000 and five players), it would be another four years before the Yankees reclaimed the American League pennant and the chance to win the World Series.

When the Yankees struck back, they did so with a vengeance. Four straight American League pennants from 1936 to 1939 gave them four trips to the World Series, all of which were won. The New York Giants were beaten 4–2 and 4–1 in 1936 and 1937; the 1936 series included an 18–4 win in game two, a record for the most runs scored in a World Series game. The Yankees had surpassed the Giants as the premier team in New York.

While the departure of Babe Ruth had allowed Lou Gehrig to step into the limelight, Gehrig had only a brief spell as the main force behind the team, for Joe DiMaggio quickly emerged as the new star. Alongside such batting luminaries as Frank Crosetti and Gehrig, catcher Bill Dickey and pitchers Red Ruffing and Lefty Gomez, DiMaggio was above everyone else, being named the league's Most Valuable Player in 1939 (Gehrig had claimed the honor in 1936), and would continue that hot streak into the following decade.

The final World Series pennant of 1939 was an especially poignant one, for the team had to play most of the season without Gehrig. The man who had earned the nickname of "the Iron Horse" had spent 17 seasons with the Yankees, setting countless records along the way, including the most career grand slams at 23 (a record that wasn't matched until 2012) and most consecutive games played (2,130); that run came to an end only when Gehrig was diagnosed with amyotrophic lateral

ABOVE: Babe Ruth slides safely past Detroit Tigers catcher Ray Hayworth in a game at Yankee Stadium during his final season for the Yankees in 1934.

FAR LEFT: Joe McCarthy with his 1938 All-Star Game players. From left to right: Lou Gehrig, Red Ruffing, Lefty Gomez, Joe DiMaggio, Bill Dickey, and Red Rolfe.

LEFT: Lou Gehrig receives the American League Most Valuable Player Award in a brief ceremony before the start of the 1935 All-Star Game.

FAR RIGHT: The "Iron Horse" of baseball says his farewells in front of 75,000 fans jammed into Yankee Stadium on July 4, 1939. Lou Gehrig gave one of the most moving speeches by an athlete, and his premature death deepened the pathos and the feeling of loss for a great American hero.

RIGHT: An emotional Babe Ruth hugs Lou Gehrig on July 4, 1939. Ruth would re-create this scene with Gary Cooper in the biopic of Gehrig's life, *Pride of the Yankees*, just three years later. The film also starred teammates Bob Meusel, Mark Koenig, and Bill Dickey, who played themselves.

BELOW: The new kid on the block, Joe DiMaggio, lets fly in his 1936 rookie season.

sclerosis, a disorder that would eventually become known as Lou Gehrig's disease.

He first reported a tendency for fatigue during the 1938 season. By the following season his play began to deteriorate, eventually leading to an extensive medical exam that revealed the illness in June 1939. A week later the Yankees announced Gehrig's retirement from the game, with the games against the Washington Senators on July 4 being proclaimed "Lou Gehrig Day." A series of presentations took place, culminating in Gehrig taking the microphone to speak to the fans.

By the end of Gehrig's speech, there was barely a dry eye left in the stadium, the crowd applauding their departing hero for fully two minutes. Gehrig would undertake a number of high-profile baseball ambassadorial roles, but nothing would have matched the sheer enjoyment he got from playing for the Yankees. Sadly, he died almost two years later, on June 2, 1941.

His wasn't the only death to hit the Yankees hard, for owner Jacob Ruppert died in January 1939, his heirs inheriting an estate of $6.3 million along with the ownership of the Yankees. Mismanagement of the estate led to the Yankees being sold to a consortium of Dan Topping, Del Webb, and Larry MacPhail in 1945 for $2.8 million.

Fans, for the past two weeks you have been reading about the bad break I got. Yet today I consider myself the luckiest man on the face of the earth. I have been in ballparks for seventeen years and have never received anything but kindness and encouragement from you fans. Look at these grand men. Which of you wouldn't consider it the highlight of his career just to associate with them for even one day? Sure, I'm lucky. Who wouldn't consider it an honor to have known Jacob Ruppert? Also, the builder of baseball's greatest empire, Ed Barrow? To have spent six years with that wonderful little fellow, Miller Huggins? Then to have spent the next nine years with that outstanding leader, that smart student of psychology, the best manager in baseball today, Joe McCarthy? Sure, I'm lucky. When the New York Giants, a team you would give your right arm to beat, and vice versa, sends you a gift—that's something. When everybody down to the groundskeepers and those boys in white coats remember you with trophies—that's something. When you have a wonderful mother-in-law who takes sides with you in squabbles with her own daughter—that's something. When you have a father and a mother who work all their lives so that you can have an education and build your body—it's a blessing. When you have a wife who has been a tower of strength and shown more courage than you dreamed existed—that's the finest I know. So I close in saying that I might have been given a bad break, but I've got an awful lot to live for. Thank you.

— Lou Gehrig at Yankee
Stadium, July 4, 1939

Lou Gehrig 4

As a player, his career was virtually unrivaled; over the course of 15 seasons from 1925 through to 1939 he played in 2,310 consecutive games, during which time he established a reputation worthy of the nickname "the Iron Horse." Even 30 years after he left the game, he was still revered, as revealed by his selection as the greatest first baseman of all time by the Baseball Writers Association in 1969.

His accomplishments were many, his reputation assured, but still the question that cannot be answered is how much greater could Lou Gehrig have become had it not been for the amyotrophic lateral sclerosis disease that struck him while he was at the height of his powers.

Born Henry Louis Gehrig in Riverdale in New York City on June 19, 1903, he had a tough upbringing, with his alcoholic father frequently out of work, leaving his mother as the chief breadwinner for the family. Lou's two sisters died at an early age, of whooping cough and measles respectively, while a brother also died in infancy. Despite these troubles, Lou's mother was adamant he would have the best possible education, and helped get him into Columbia University in 1921 on a football scholarship to pursue an engineering degree.

He played baseball under an assumed name in summer professional games, but was banned from intercollegiate sports for a year after being discovered playing for Hartford in the Eastern League. In spite of his football prowess, it was baseball that attracted outside interest, first for the Columbia Nine and then on his return to Hartford. Yankees manager Miller Huggins was convinced of Lou's abilities and would eventually sign him in 1925 as a potential replacement for the aging Wally Pipp at first base; once Gehrig got in, he didn't leave the field for over 13 years, playing a remarkable 2,310 consecutive games.

TOP: Gehrig whacks a double into left center in a game at Yankee Stadium in 1938. Luke Sewell is the catcher for the Chicago White Sox.

ABOVE: Lou with his wife Eleanor at Yankee Stadium before a game against Washington in April 1937. It was Eleanor who called the Mayo Clinic in Minnesota to diagnose Gehrig's rapid loss of strength and coordination.

His consecutive-game tally remained a record for nearly 60 years, but there were several occasions when the run might have been brought to a halt; Lou played games with a broken thumb, broken toe, and severe back spasms. When he was sent for X-rays later in his career, the results showed that he had suffered 17 different fractures that had healed themselves over the course of his career!

Alongside Babe Ruth, Lou Gehrig turned the New York Yankees into the dominant force in Major League Baseball, winning six World Series in 11 years. And if Ruth was seen as the face of the Yankees for much of that time, then someone forgot to tell the rest of the baseball world about it; Gehrig was named Most Valuable Player on two occasions during that same spell. He also earned seven straight selections to the All-Star Game from 1933 to 1939.

The first sign that his abilities were failing came during the 1938 season. A poor first half was turned around later in the season, but by the end of the campaign Gehrig revealed he had tired midway through and had struggled to get going. At spring training camp he collapsed, and the deterioration of his running and coordination had become marked. A few games into the 1939 season, Gehrig took the decision to bench himself, feeling he was contributing little or nothing to the team. In an effort to locate the root of the problem, he visited a clinic for extensive tests in June 1939. After six days, the results revealed lateral sclerosis (which has since become known as Lou Gehrig's disease) and the immediate end of his baseball career. His wife Eleanor kept the full diagnosis from him, and while Gehrig thought he might decline over a period of ten to fifteen years, perhaps needing a cane to walk, in reality the experts had given him three years to live.

His departure from Yankee Stadium was one of the most emotional the venue had ever witnessed, with the attendant crowd and players in tears as Gehrig bade his farewell with profound dignity. The Yankees retired his number 4 jersey, the first player in Major League Baseball history to be afforded that honor. A couple of months later he accepted an offer from New York mayor Fiorello La Guardia and began a planned 10-year term as a New York City parole commissioner, although the continuing worsening of his physical condition meant that by May 1941 his hand had to be guided when he signed his name.

Sixteen years to the day that he had replaced Wally Pipp at first base, Lou Gehrig died at his home on June 2, 1941. The mayor ordered all the flags in New York to be flown at half-mast, and major league ballparks would follow suit. A monument to him was erected at Yankee Stadium the following month and placed next to the tribute to manager Miller Huggins. He was elected to the Baseball Hall of Fame, and the following year Gary Cooper (an uncanny fit as Gehrig) starred as Gehrig in *The Pride of the Yankees*, which would earn 11 Academy Award nominations. In death, just as in life, Lou Gehrig took center stage.

ABOVE: Joe DiMaggio famously wed Marilyn Monroe in 1954. Before that, however, he married another actress, Dorothy Arnold, in November 1939 in San Francisco. DiMaggio met Arnold on the set of the movie *Manhattan Merry-Go-Round*, where he had a small role and she was an extra. This publicity photo shows the newlyweds reluctantly saying good-bye as Joe packs his glove to travel to New York for the start of the season.

WIVES AND GIRLFRIENDS

Baseball stars have often married childhood sweethearts and actresses

ABOVE: Babe Ruth's first marriage, at age 19, was to the shy and retiring Helen Woodford. As his fame increased, Ruth found women throwing themselves at him, and his serial infidelities contributed to the breakdown of the marriage. The couple separated in 1926, but as both were

Catholics, divorce was not an option. Unlike today, newspapers refrained from reporting celebrities' affairs. Helen died in a fire in 1929. In the meantime, Ruth began seeing Claire Merritt Hodgson, shown here with him prior to a game at Yankee Stadium in 1930. She became his second

wife in April 1929. Claire came from money and, being strong-willed, helped curb Ruth's excesses. She even persuaded Yankees owner Jacob Ruppert to pay for her to share a hotel room with her husband when the team was on the road, to keep him away from "distractions."

ABOVE: Merlyn and Mickey Mantle smile for the cameras after leaving Yankee Stadium on April 26, 1965. Sadly, both would be troubled by alcoholism after Mantle's retirement from the game.

BELOW: Yogi and Carmen Berra, just weeks after their marriage in 1949, in St. Petersburg, Florida. Though it doesn't look it, Yogi was upset with the new contract he'd been offered after an impressive 1948 season. He claimed that marriage gave him new responsibilities and a need for more money.

RIGHT: Yankees shortstop Derek Jeter and girlfriend Minka Kelly in November 2009. Baseball players now share the gossip columns and tabloids with stars from the entertainment industry. Madonna, Cameron Diaz, and Kate Hudson all dated third baseman Alex Rodriguez, and actress Joanna Garcia married outfielder Nick Swisher.

BELOW: The end of an era and a moment shared, Mariano Rivera walks in from the bullpen with his wife Clara long after the final game at the old Yankee Stadium on September 21, 2008, in which the Yankees played the Orioles. Mariano and Clara were childhood sweethearts and met at elementary school in Panama.

BABE RUTH HITS HIS 700TH HOME RUN

One of Babe Ruth's ambitions for 1934 was to become the first player to reach the career total of 700 home runs. At the time, Lou Gehrig and Rogers Hornsby were the only two other players in baseball with 300 career home runs. In 1921, his eighth season, Ruth had surpassed the previous mark of 139 homers, set by Roger Connor.

History might have been different had the Yankees released Ruth from his playing contract so he could take up an offer to manage the Cincinnati Reds in December 1933. They refused, and in January 1934 the Sultan of Swat agreed a new one-year deal worth $35,000.

The season began with the Babe on 686 career homers. Although he was nearing the end of his playing days at 39 years of age, the magic 700 figure seemed within his grasp. He played in 125 games that season, but manager Joe McCarthy tended to rest him toward the end of games, sending in Myril Hoag or Sammy Bird to take his place. He was also dogged by a knee injury caused when he was hit by a pitch. In June he suffered an 0-for-24 slump but was still selected to appear for the second straight year for the American League in the All-Star Game, where he was one of five consecutive strikeout victims claimed by New York Giants pitcher Carl Hubbell.

The Babe wrote another chapter in baseball history during a midseason game in Detroit. The Yankees were facing the Tigers in the

ABOVE: Leonard Beals gets an autographed ball and $20 from the Babe for returning his 700th home run ball.

second of a four-game series. At Nevin Field on Friday, July 13, 1934, a crowd of 21,000 watched in the second inning as Ruth, wearing the familiar number 3, faced right-handed curveball specialist Tommy Bridges, one of the best pitchers in the game. He made clean contact with the ball; it cleared the bleachers and flew over the right-field wall, landing on the street behind. Babe Ruth's 700th homer is estimated to have traveled more than 500 feet.

A young boy, Leonard Beals, retrieved the ball and brought it back to Ruth. The slugger paid $20 to Beals so he could add it to his collection. This was widely reported in the press and drew parallels with a similar incident three years earlier, when he hit number 600 in St. Louis. On that occasion, two kids brought balls to Ruth, both claiming that they were the Babe's, and he paid $10 for each ball. Similarly, five years earlier, he had paid $10 for his 500th home run ball.

The Yankees emerged victorious, but it was to be their only win in the four-game series against the Tigers, who would ultimately claim the pennant, seven games ahead of the Yankees. Babe Ruth hit another homer the following day, although the Yankees lost that game.

There were other, perhaps more poignant, milestones for the Babe as the season drew to a close. During his last game at Yankee Stadium, Ruth went 0 for 3 against the Boston Red Sox on September 24. Six days later at Washington's Griffith Stadium, he wore the pinstripes for the last time as the Yankees went down 5–3 to the Senators. The Babe finished the season with 22 homers, the eighth-best total in the league. Lou Gehrig's 49 home runs was the best in the majors that year. Ruth achieved a batting average of .288 and drove in 84 runs. His career total at the end of the 1934 season was 708 home runs.

BELOW LEFT: Babe Ruth scores in the third inning on Bill Dickey's single, securing the first game of a doubleheader between the Yankees and the Tigers at Yankee Stadium on August 15, 1934.

BELOW: In his brief spell with the Boston Braves in 1935, Ruth took the home run mark to 714. Only two men have achieved the same feat since: Hank Aaron in 1973 (755) and Barry Bonds in 2004 (762). However, the Sultan of Swat reached 700 faster than the others, and did it in 1,000 fewer at bats than Aaron.

Bill Dickey

One of the stars of the early 20th century, Bill Dickey is considered to be among the best catchers to have ever graced the field. His record of helping the Yankees reach nine World Series (and winning eight of them) is a testament to his skill and dedication to both the club and the sport of baseball.

Born in Bastrop, Louisiana, on June 6, 1907, William Malcolm Dickey moved with his family to Kensett, Arkansas, when he was 15 years old. He was one of seven children, and the lure of baseball was strong in his family: his father John and older brother Gus played semiprofessionally while his younger brother George later became a catcher for the Boston Red Sox and Chicago White Sox. Dickey's first taste of baseball came at Searcy High School, where he was a pitcher and second baseman before moving on to Little Rock College. Dickey gained valuable experience playing for a semiprofessional team in Hot Springs, and it was there that his natural talents were spotted. He was soon signed to play for the Little Rock Travelers, making his minor league debut at the age of 18.

Little Rock had an arrangement with the Chicago White Sox that gave its players the chance to play for the Muskogee Athletics (Class C Western Association) and the Jackson Senators (Class D Cotton States League). It had been anticipated that the White Sox would take up Dickey's contract, but he slipped through their fingers and was promptly signed by the Yankees, who paid the Jackson Senators the princely sum of $12,500 and assigned him to Little Rock for the 1928 season.

Dickey's progress was meteoric and—after just three games for the Buffalo Bisons in the Class AA International League—he made his major league debut on August 15, 1928, when the Yankees faced the St. Louis Browns. The following season, Dickey replaced Benny Bengough as the starting catcher, and he never

looked back. The rookie finished as the best catcher with 95 assists and 13 double plays while recording a batting average of .324, with 10 home runs and 65 runs batted in. By the end of his playing career, Dickey had set numerous records, including catching 100 or more games for 13 successive seasons. Indeed, it was only a shoulder injury suffered during the 1942 season that prevented him from extending his record. His first success at the

LEFT: Bill Dickey poses for the cameras prior to the 1941 World Series.

BELOW: At the 1937 All-Star Game at Griffith Stadium in Washington, D.C., from left to right: Lou Gehrig, Joe Cronin, Bill Dickey, Joe DiMaggio, Charley Gehringer, Jimmie Foxx, and Hank Greenberg.

World Series was in 1932, and he helped the Yankees to seven more titles (1936–39 and 1941–43). His 38 games played in the World Series culminated with the winning home run against the Cardinals in 1943. He also played in 11 All-Star Games between 1933 and 1946, and his lifetime batting average of .313 (in 1,789 games) included 202 home runs and 1,209 runs batted in.

Dickey's success was partially attributed to his size—being 6 feet 2 inches tall and weighing more than 180 pounds meant he was larger than many of his contemporaries—but mainly to his skills, especially durability and hitting. He was adept at handling pitchers, and his throwing arm was extremely strong and accurate. He was the first catcher to go a complete season (1931) with no passed balls, and was a pioneer of one-handed catching.

World War II meant a hiatus for Dickey's baseball career, and he enlisted in the navy in 1944, returning in 1946 and becoming player-manager following Joe McCarthy's departure. He retired at the end of the season and briefly managed the Little Rock Travelers before returning to the Yankees, this time in a coaching role. One of his protégés was a young catcher who would go on to become one of the greatest players of all time, Yogi Berra. Dickey helped the Yankees to another six World Series titles, and was inducted into the National Baseball Hall of Fame in 1954. The number 8 he was associated with was retired by the Yankees in 1972 in honor of both Dickey and his successor Yogi Berra.

Dickey left baseball to work for an investment firm before enjoying a well-earned retirement, although he suffered a stroke in 1989 that left him housebound. Dickey died at the age of 86 in Little Rock on November 12, 1993, and was buried in the town's Roselawn Cemetery.

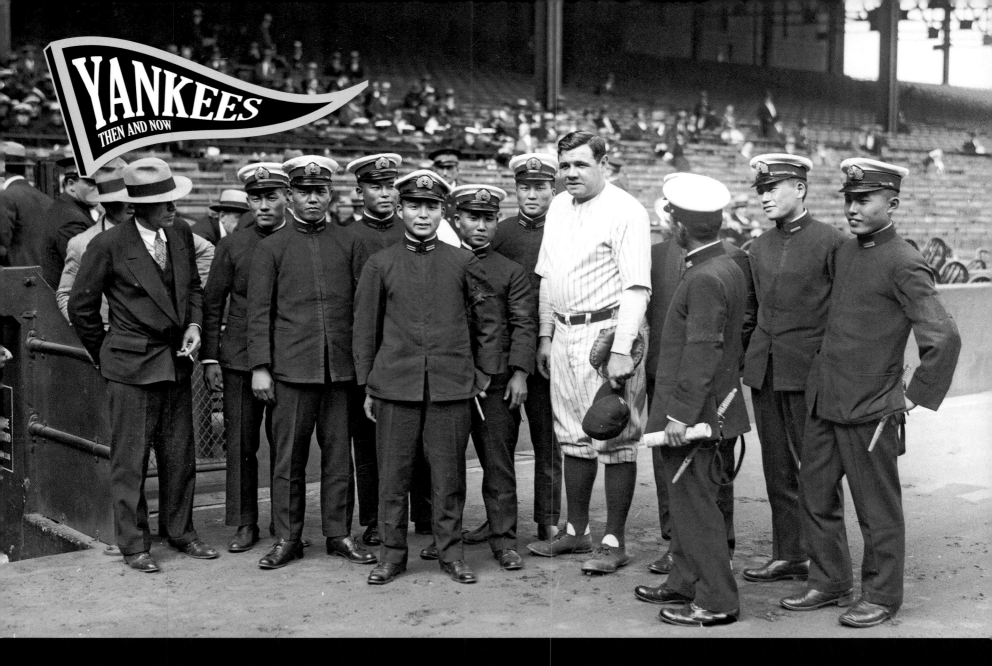

BIG IN JAPAN

Babe Ruth helped make the Yankees and baseball big in Japan—and now Japan is big in baseball

ABOVE: In the spring of 1927, officers of the Japanese fleet docked in New York Harbor and were invited to watch a game at Yankee Stadium. They were impressed by the slugging power of Babe Ruth, who marked the occasion with two home runs, one with the bases loaded. Ever the showman, the Babe proceeded to entertain the Japanese visitors by drawing a short sword from an officer's sheath and testing the sharpness of the blade on a baseball. He also playfully put the sword to his own throat. Ruth is shown here with the officers, who were amused at his antics. Ruth would later visit Japan, where he quickly became a popular figure.

ABOVE: In November 1950, Joe DiMaggio and coach Lefty O'Doul visited Japan for a barnstorming tour to promote baseball in the country. Here, DiMaggio teaches youngsters to bat at Korakua Stadium in Tokyo.

RIGHT: Ichiro Suzuki in a game against the Baltimore Orioles at Yankee Stadium on September 2, 2012.

BELOW: Babe Ruth signs a baseball for Emperor Hirohito and his wife before a game at Yankee Stadium in 1930.

ABOVE: Baseball had been popular in Japan since the late 19th century, but the efforts of visiting American stars like DiMaggio and Ruth helped to establish the professional game there. The first Japanese player in Major League Baseball was Masanori Marakami of the San Francisco Giants in 1964. The first Japanese player to wear a Yankee uniform, Hideki Irabu, was actually of mixed Asian and American heritage. He signed in 1997 after starting his career in his country's Pacific League and wore the pinstripes between 2003 and 2009. The 2012 Yankees roster included two players from Japan, pitcher Hiroki Kuroda and outfielder Ichiro Suzuki, who was obtained from the Seattle Mariners in a trade that year. Less successful was Kei Igawa, a star pitcher in his homeland, who signed a $20 million contract with the Yankees in January 2007 but was soon sent to the minors after some disappointing performances.

JOE DIMAGGIO IS ACQUIRED FROM SAN FRANCISCO

ABOVE: Joe DiMaggio photographed October 6, 1936.

Joe DiMaggio grew up playing baseball on the sandlots of North Beach in San Francisco, near where his father worked as a fisherman. Two of Joe's brothers, Vince and Dominic, also became pro baseball players, but Joe was the most talented of the lot.

Vince was on the roster for the Pacific Coast League's San Francisco Seals and suggested that Joe be signed when a vacancy for shortstop arose. Joe made his professional debut in April 1932, and played three games that season. During his first full season in minor league baseball, the 20-year-old DiMaggio attracted the attention of major league scouts with a hitting streak that lasted for an amazing 61 games. During his rookie season he batted .340 with 169 RBIs and 28 home runs.

History could have turned out differently. In the off-season between 1934 and 1935, the Seals offered Joe DiMaggio to the Chicago Cubs. However, he was suffering from torn ligaments in his left knee, sustained while getting out of a cab, and the Cubs didn't want to risk parting with money for a player who was not fully fit. Seals owner Charlie Graham, who had been hoping to sell DiMaggio for $100,000, tried to keep the deal alive with a revised offer. He would allow DiMaggio to join the Cubs for spring training in 1935, and if he wasn't fully recovered the Seals would take him back. Cubs chief Philip K. Wrigley was not convinced. He decided that an outfield that boasted Chuck Klein, Kiki Cuyler, and Augie Galan was strong enough and declined the offer, to the everlasting chagrin of Cubs fans. At first it seemed that Wrigley may have called it right, as the Cubs went to the World Series in 1935, but lost to the Detroit Tigers. DiMaggio would lead the Yankees to glory the next year.

The knee injury was of concern to the Yankees, too, but scout Bill Esick persuaded the club that Joe could overcome the injury. After DiMaggio passed a medical, the Yankees and Seals agreed to a fee of just $25,000 and Joe became a Yankee on November 21, 1935. He was loaned back to

the Seals for the remainder of their 1935 campaign.

After their sweep of the Chicago Cubs in the 1932 World Series, the Yankees had finished second in the American League for three consecutive years. Babe Ruth played his last game as a Yankee in 1934. The team still had plenty of star players but were sorely in need of a young star. DiMaggio proved to be just that in his rookie season. His much-anticipated debut came a month into the season on May 3, 1936, when the Yankees faced the St. Louis Browns at Yankee Stadium. DiMaggio collected three hits in a 14–5 victory for the home side. Led by DiMaggio, the Yankees cruised to the division title by 19½ games, finishing with a record of 102–51. Joe played 138 games and boasted an average of .323. He was second to Lou Gehrig in home runs with 29, and added 125 RBIs as well.

BELOW: The "Italian hit men (via San Francisco)" gathered together for a press photo before the 1936 World Series. From left to right are Frank Crosetti, Tony Lazzeri, and Joe DiMaggio. The Yankees reclaimed the series with a 4–2 win over the New York Giants. DiMaggio hit .346, and his heroics also included a remarkable catch in deep center field.

Joe DiMaggio (5)

Joe DiMaggio was not only one of the greatest players of all time, but a man who was a New York Yankee through and through. He was a team player who still achieved many personal milestones at the plate. His 13-year career with the Yankees brought unrivaled success, including no less than 10 American League pennants and nine World Series titles.

Giuseppe Paolo "Joe" DiMaggio was born in Martinez, California, at the end of 1914. He was the eighth of nine children born to Giuseppe Sr. and Rosalie, who had emigrated from Sicily. The DiMaggios were a family of fishermen, and Joe seemed destined to follow in their footsteps, but he hated the smell of fish and loathed cleaning fishing boats even more! So when he was introduced to baseball at 10 years old, it appeared the perfect opportunity to escape the family business.

What began as a way to duck out of the fishing trade quickly became a career path for Joe when his brother Vince was signed by the minor league San Francisco Seals and began bringing home the dollars. Joe wanted a piece of the action, and it was Vince who helped get him a place on the team, initially filling in at shortstop. It was all the opportunity Joe needed; his talent did the rest, and he was promptly signed up on a full-time basis.

Among his early performances for the Seals at bat, DiMaggio showed glimpses of what was to come in his career with a 61-game hitting streak in his first full season. Despite a potentially career-ending knee injury, some of the biggest names in baseball turned their attentions to San Francisco in 1935. The Yankees snapped up the 22-year-old for $25,000 plus some five players—and while the Seals were grateful for the cash, their hottest prospect would prove impossible to replace. As he recovered from his knee injury, he stayed with the Seals for an extra season, smashing 34 home runs and

proving that rumors of his demise were greatly exaggerated.

DiMaggio joined the Yankees after the Babe Ruth years, enduring what was then considered a barren spell of four years without an American League pennant. Alongside future Hall of Famers like Lou Gehrig and Lefty Gomez, the Yankees were propelled to the pennant and a World Series victory over the Giants in 1936. It would be the first of four consecutive World Series, with DiMaggio hitting a home run in the 1937 series, again versus the Giants. Wins against the Chicago Cubs and Cincinnati Reds followed in 1938 and 1939, making DiMaggio the only player to win four World Series in his first four years in the majors.

While there was to be no World Series appearance in 1940, the following year would see the Yankees return to the top, with DiMaggio having the season of his career. It was the year Joe attracted the attention of the nation with a sequence that would become known across the years as simply "the streak." Beginning in May 1941 against the Chicago White Sox, DiMaggio's 56-game hitting streak lasted until July, smashing George Sisler's record of 41 games, set in 1922. To this day, no one has surpassed DiMaggio's streak; many claim that no one ever will. To cap it off, DiMaggio compiled a batting average of .357, with 30 home runs. It came as no surprise when he was awarded the American League MVP for the second time at the season's close.

After the triumph came reality. DiMaggio, like so many others, was enlisted to the U.S. Army in 1943 to serve in World War II. He returned in 1945 on medical grounds, having served at a California air base and a brief stint in Hawaii. He suited up again for the Yankees in 1947 and, just like his first

RIGHT: In a game from his 1936 rookie season, DiMaggio rips a single up the middle against the Cleveland Indians.

season, led the team to the World Series, toppling the Brooklyn Dodgers. DiMaggio hit three homers during the seven-game series.

Though the Yankees had captured one wartime World Series in 1943, DiMaggio's return heralded more consistent successes, with three World Series titles between 1949 and 1951. But while his stats suggested otherwise, Joe's career was winding down. Chronic pain in his heel caused him to hang up his bat in 1951 at the age of 37. The number 5 he wore on the back of his jersey was retired by the Yankees the following year.

DiMaggio's life outside the diamond was just as much public interest as his career inside it. Briefly

wed in the 1940s to actress Dorothy Arnold, it was DiMaggio's second marriage that set America talking. A retired DiMaggio met actress Marilyn Monroe in 1952, and they would embark on a whirlwind relationship that culminated in what the media dubbed "the marriage of the century" in 1954. But the relationship would not last, the pair divorcing less than a year later. They remained close friends, and Joe would deliver roses to Monroe's grave for 20 years after her death. He was subsequently immortalized as an American sporting icon in Paul Simon's song "Mrs. Robinson" with the lyrics "Where have you gone, Joe DiMaggio, a nation turns its lonely eyes to you"—a sentiment much echoed by Yankee fans when the song was released in 1968.

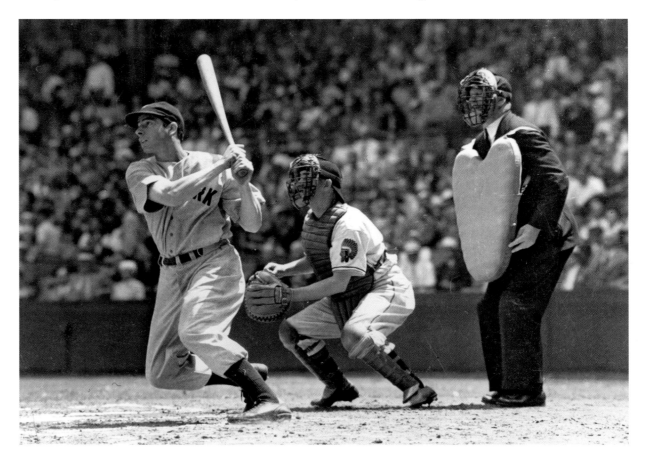

ABOVE: Jerry Coleman (left) and Phil Rizzuto were once infielders for the Yankees, but this argument, separated by umpires Carolyn Larson, Elsie Lindauer, and Holly Hill at Yankee Stadium, came long after their playing days were over. Coleman and Rizzuto were a broadcasting team from 1963 to 1969.

BELOW: Shortly after the Yankees' 1928 World Series victory, Lou Gehrig and Babe Ruth promote the World Series Rodeo (now known as the National Finals Rodeo) at Dexter Park in Queens on October 13, 1928. Gehrig would go on to star in his own cowboy film, *Rawhide*, which premiered in St. Petersburg, Florida, in March 1938 while the Yankees were in town for spring training. City boy Gehrig joked that it was the first time he'd ever sat on a horse.

![Yankees Then and Now pennant]

CLOWNING AROUND

George Steinbrenner was not a fan of mascots

ABOVE: Baseball is generally a serious business, but sometimes there is room for comedy in or around the ballpark, either with mascots or the offbeat photo opportunity. That was the case in 1929. James "One Eye" Connelly was the world's most famous gate-crasher, notorious for his uncanny ability to sneak into sporting events and political conventions unnoticed. Here Babe Ruth delivers the bum's rush to Connelly on the New York Yankees' training field in St. Petersburg, Florida.

ABOVE: Washington Senators pitcher Al Schacht's abilities as a mimic and his comedy routines earned him the nickname "the Clown Prince of Baseball." Before the second game of the World Series on October 5, 1939, he clowns with Joe DiMaggio at Yankee Stadium.

TOP RIGHT: Former St. Louis Cardinals player and Yankees manager Joe Torre was one of the guests invited to change the numbers in the countdown to the opening of the Cardinals' new Busch Stadium in 2005. Here he rides in a buggy with the popular Cardinals mascot Fredbird on June 11, 2005. In the serious business of the game, the Yankees won 5–0.

RIGHT: Hideki Matsui shares a joke with the New York Mets' Mr. Met—baseball's first live mascot—in 2003. The Yankees are one of only four MLB teams without a mascot. From 1979 to 1981, the role was fulfilled by a character named "Dandy," created by Acme Mascots, the people behind the popular Phillie Phanatic. Dandy was a mustachioed, pinstriped bird named after the song "Yankee Doodle Dandy." The character was unpopular with fans, and when the three-year deal expired, it was not renewed. Acme claimed the mascot did not receive the necessary support from Yankee management. Certainly owner George Steinbrenner wasn't sitting on the fence after the San Diego Padres' Chicken enraged Lou Piniella before a game in 1979. Steinbrenner told the press that mascots had no place in baseball. Dandy, who started just weeks later, was confined to the upper deck. David Raymond performed as the original Phillie Phanatic and had sympathy for Dandy. "I remember what it was like in the upper deck in Philadelphia. That's why I never went up there. When you go up into the upper deck, they want to see if you really can fly."

⭐ **The Yankees slumped to third place in the** American League in 1940, their lowest placing in 10 years, but Joe McCarthy went to work on the team to ensure that the slump was merely an aberration, as the team reclaimed the pennant at the end of the 1941 season. They carried on that form into the World Series, beating the Brooklyn

Dodgers 4–1. Yet far greater battles lay ahead, for in December 1941 the Japanese made their surprise attack on Pearl Harbor.

While Major League Baseball would continue for the duration of the war, it often did so without the contributions of well-known Yankees players, who

either enlisted or got called up to don a different kind of uniform. Chief among those who served their country was Joe DiMaggio. His value to the Yankees was obvious, culminating in his still-unbeaten record of recording a hit in 56 consecutive games. Over 13 seasons he hit 361 home runs and was named the Most Valuable

Player three times; he is considered one of the best center fielders of all time.

Another who put his playing career on hold was Lawrence Peter "Yogi" Berra. Spotted playing in the minor leagues, Berra seemed destined to sign for the St. Louis Cardinals in 1942, but they opted to sign his boyhood best friend Joe Garagiola instead. It was later revealed that Cardinals team president Branch Rickey was impressed with Berra and planned to sign him to the Brooklyn Dodgers, where Rickey would soon be headed. The Yankees stepped in first and were able to sign Berra for $500, loaning him out to the Norfolk Tars of the Class B Piedmont League. He soon signed up with the U.S. Navy and saw action during the war, including time as a gunner's mate during the D-Day landings at Normandy.

While the Yankees had to continue without several of their key players, their domination of the game continued. They won the American League again in 1942 but were beaten 4–1 in the World Series by the St. Louis Cardinals, even though Joe Gordon was named Most Valuable Player. The following year it was Spud Chandler who took center stage, anchoring the team's pitching staff with a 20–4 record as the Yankees won their third consecutive pennant; Chandler became the only Yankees pitcher to win the Most Valuable Player Award. He would also have the most successful World Series of his career, pitching two complete-game victories, including

a shutout in game five as the Yankees gained their revenge on the Cardinals with a 4–1 victory.

That victory served to herald the end of another Yankees era, for it would be another three years before they won the American League again. It had been fully 10 years since the Yankees had gone as long as three years between pennants, and early in 1946 their patience finally ran out; Joe McCarthy was let go. A couple of interim managers came and went, with stability finally being restored with the appointment of Bucky Harris in 1947.

After winning the American League, the Yankees came up against the Brooklyn Dodgers in the World Series, emerging triumphant in seven games. Unfortunately, co-owner Larry MacPhail got into several confrontations at the postgame celebrations, which threatened to spoil the victory. As a result, his partners Dan Topping and Del Webb forced a buyout to remove MacPhail from the club.

The Yankees were unable to retain their crown the following year and, despite only finishing three games behind the Cleveland Indians, Bucky Harris was released. In his place came Casey Stengel, whose appointment raised more than a few eyebrows. While the Yankees had enjoyed most of their success with disciplinarians at the helm, Stengel was seen as something of a maverick. Yet he was confident he could turn the ship around.

Despite Stengel's confidence, the Yankees went into the 1949 season facing an uphill battle because the Boston Red Sox were favored to win the pennant. Somehow the Yankees overtook the Red Sox on the final two days of the season, putting in place a traditional rivalry that continues to this day. After their strenuous efforts during the regular season, the Yankees beat the Dodgers in the World Series in five games.

LEFT: Joe DiMaggio served as a staff sergeant in the U.S. Army Air Force between 1943 and 1945.

FAR LEFT: The original caption from October 4, 1943, reads: "Catcher Bill Dickey (left) and pitcher Spud Chandler will be the battery of the New York Yankees for the opening game of the World Series against the St. Louis Cardinals at Yankee Stadium tomorrow. Dickey is a veteran of many series classics, Chandler has won 20 games for the Yanks this season."

BELOW: As a publicist and promoter of his teams, Casey Stengel had no equal. When he arrived at Yankee Stadium, he observed, "There is less wrong with this team than any team I have ever managed."

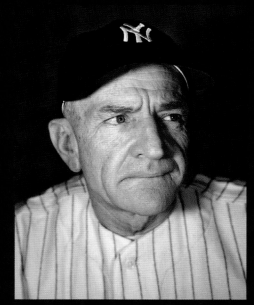

JOE DIMAGGIO'S STREAK ENDS AT 56

ABOVE: Game 56: DiMaggio slides safely past Indians catcher Gene Desautes to register one of the runs that beat Cleveland 10–3.

The sight of Joe DiMaggio at the plate was a daunting prospect for opposing pitchers. But one of the greatest baseball milestones began quietly on May 15, 1941, at Yankee Stadium when DiMaggio hit a single against the Chicago White Sox in a game that the Yankees ultimately lost 13–1. The next day, the Bronx Bombers bounced back with a 6–5 victory. DiMaggio went 2 for 4, including a massive home run and a ninth-inning triple to set up the win. The game marked the point where the Yankees, inspired by DiMaggio's prowess with a bat, recovered from an early season slump and advanced toward World Series glory. The streak continued in a third contest against the White Sox.

On May 27, 1941, the day before game 13 of DiMaggio's streak, President Franklin D. Roosevelt announced an unlimited national emergency in response to threats from Nazi Germany. Many of the players in the Yankees–Senators game thought they could be drafted. In the next game of the series, Senators pitcher Smokey Sundra struck out DiMaggio in the first inning, but the Yankee Clipper kept the streak alive with a single in the fourth.

A doubleheader against the rival Boston Red Sox pitted Joe not only against his younger brother Dom but also against star Red Sox hitter Ted Williams. The streak reached 16 as the Yankees won the first game 6–5 but lost the second.

DiMaggio's exploits were now starting to attract attention, but were overshadowed by the news of Lou Gehrig's death on June 2. After reaching 24 during a doubleheader at St. Louis, it became national news. DiMaggio continued the streak against the Chicago White Sox as New York won four in a row to move into second place. They narrowed the gap to one game after a three-game series against division leaders Cleveland when DiMaggio reached 29, equaling the previous best for a Yankee player. It was extended to 30 the next day with a controversial hit awarded by the official scorer.

By June, Joltin' Joe was the talk of the nation as he closed in on George Sisler's American League record of 41. Sisler's mark was tied and surpassed on June 29 in a doubleheader at Washington. The next target was Willie Keeler's all-time record of 44. That fell against Boston at Yankee Stadium in early July. Both on the road and at Yankee Stadium, the Yankees—now in first place—attracted big crowds eager to see history in the making. The streak seemed destined to last forever, reaching 56 at League Park in the opening game of a crucial three-game series against Cleveland. The next day, Cleveland switched venues to the larger Municipal Stadium. On the evening of July 17, 1941, the biggest crowd of the season watched as DiMaggio went 0 for 3. The streak was over, but the Yankees won the game.

The magnitude of DiMaggio's record has become more apparent over time. Babe Ruth's record of 60 home runs stood for 34 years, while Roger Maris's 61 endured for 37 years. DiMaggio's record has been untouched for more than 70 years; the closest anyone has come was Pete Rose's 44-game streak in 1978. It is considered a record that will likely never be broken.

ABOVE: If he wasn't already, the streak made DiMaggio a national sporting hero.

BELOW LEFT: July 18, 1941: the streak is over. Joe DiMaggio signals a double zero as his 57th game ends hitless. He went 0 for 4 but managed to reach base on a walk.

BELOW: The headline from July 3, after DiMaggio topped the previous record.

LOU GEHRIG AND BABE RUTH PLAZAS

The "House that Ruth Built" may be gone now, but his plaza remains

LEFT: At the newly renamed Lou Gehrig Plaza on April 30, 1942, Eleanor Gehrig unveiled the plaque to the memory of her husband, who died on June 2, 1941. From left to right in this photo are Yankees catcher (and Gehrig's longtime road roommate) Bill Dickey, Lou's parents Henry and Christina Gehrig, Joe McCarthy, Eleanor Gehrig, and Bronx borough president James J. Lyons. Bill Dickey once said, "Lou didn't need tributes from anyone. His life and the way he lived were tribute enough."

LEFT: Lou Gehrig Plaza remains in its original location, now one block from the new Yankee Stadium on East 161st Street, where it forms part of a gateway to fans approaching the stadium from that side. The plaza lies on the Grand Concourse, sometimes called the "Champs-Elysées of the Bronx" after the Parisian boulevard on which it was modeled. The concourse runs for four miles through the heart of the Bronx, and Gehrig Plaza was refurbished as part of a major scheme coinciding with the construction of the new Yankee Stadium. Like the Babe Ruth marker, the plaque underwent restoration and required much cosmetic repair, including the addition of a new bronze baseball to replace the original, which was missing from the center of the plaque.

ABOVE AND BELOW: The new Babe Ruth Plaza, seen here in September 2012, is situated outside the new Yankee Stadium on the south (right-field) side between gates 4 and 6. A series of storyboards and porcelain images tell the life story of the Babe. The bronze plaque was repaired and restored in 2008 during the construction of the new Yankee Stadium.

ABOVE: A year after his death from cancer, the world of baseball honored the memory of Babe Ruth with silences at games. In New York, two tree-lined blocks situated to the rear of Yankee Stadium were renamed Babe Ruth Plaza at a dedication ceremony on August 18, 1949. Shown here is the marker for the plaza in its original location at the intersection of 161st Street and River Avenue. A crowd of 5,000 watched the event, which was also attended by Joe DiMaggio and the entire Yankees roster in uniform, along with manager Casey Stengel and Ruth's widow, Claire.

THE FRIEZE

The design element that made Yankee Stadium instantly recognizable in press photos

LEFT: The fact that the original Yankee Stadium was conceived as something more than an ordinary baseball venue was evident in the frieze. This gently curving latticework ran around the roof of the grandstand and was commissioned by owners Jacob Ruppert and Cap Huston to give the stadium an air of dignity. It was made of copper and, over the years, it took on a green patina; to disguise this, the frieze was given a few coats of white paint in the 1960s. When plans for a refurbished stadium were drawn up in 1973, Yankees chief executive Michael Burke was surprised to be told that the frieze could not be accommodated in the new grandstand. Incoming owner George Steinbrenner arrived too late to alter the plans. Instead, a replica was installed behind the outfield fence above the bleachers and the scoreboard. The design of the frieze was so utterly distinctive and original that it became inextricably identified with the Yankees; versions were added to the locker rooms of both the refurbished and new stadiums. Its removal in the 1970s came to be viewed as a mistake, and the club was able to atone for this during construction of the new stadium.

LEFT: A different kind of Bronx Bomber flies over Yankee Stadium during game two of the 1943 World Series.

ABOVE AND LEFT: The frieze now encircles the top deck of the grandstand in the new stadium. It is made of steel coated with zinc, and is painted white. Although it looks similar to its predecessor, closer examination reveals that the design is less intricate. It consists of 38 connected panels that are 11 feet deep, 12 feet high, and 40 feet long. The frieze weighs in at 315 tons and forms an integral part of the support structure of the grandstand roof. It does not, however, project out of the roof to the same extent as the original.

CASEY STENGEL TAKES OVER AS MANAGER

Casey Stengel's initial spells in Major League Baseball management in the 1930s and early 1940s with the Brooklyn Dodgers and the Boston Braves were not notably successful. He returned to the minor leagues where his managerial career had first begun, making a name for himself with the Milwaukee Brewers. He led them to the American Association pennant in 1944 and then won the Pacific Coast League championship with the Oakland Oaks in 1948.

At the time, the Yankees were looking for a new manager. Bucky Harris had piloted them to the World Series in 1947 but was fired after a disappointing sophomore season, when the team could only muster third place in the American League. Stengel's exploits in Oakland attracted the attention of the Yankees, and on October 12, 1948, to the general disbelief of the baseball world, the Yankees announced that the 58-year-old had been appointed as the new manager.

Stengel's eccentric public image was at the root of much of the skepticism. But behind the clownish facade lay a deep knowledge of baseball, stemming from his lengthy, if unspectacular, career as a player. Nearly 25 years of management experience helped his standing. The media grew to love Stengel because of his unique world view, sense of humor, and ability to talk entertainingly about baseball, or any subject for that matter; his musings became known as "Stengelese." His facility with a one-liner was unmatched. On management, he said, "The key to being a good manager is keeping the people who hate me away from those who are still undecided."

The Yankees' performance in 1949 silenced Stengel's critics. He proceeded to guide the team to the division pennant and then the world championship. Along the route, Stengel showed himself to be an unparalleled

LEFT: The old campaigner at spring training in 1956.

tactician, especially in the virtually lost art of platooning left- and right-handed hitters.

During that year, the Yankees were seen as underdogs, and their season was blighted by injuries. The race for the league pennant was a close contest between the Yankees and the Red Sox. The final series of the season brought the two teams head-to-head at Yankee Stadium, with Boston needing only one win in two games to take the title and progress to the World Series, which they had narrowly missed out on the previous year after a playoff with the Cleveland Indians. To add spice to the mix, the Red Sox were managed by former Yankees chief Joe McCarthy.

The Yankees had little margin for error, but as Stengel once remarked, "Never make predictions, especially about the future." After trailing 4–0 in the first game, the Bronx Bombers pulled of a remarkable comeback to win 5–4 with Johnny Lindell hitting a game-winning home run in the eighth inning. "Managing is getting paid for home runs someone else hits," said Stengel. Both teams now had records of 96–57, and it was all down to the last game of the season. The next day saw the Yankees survive a ninth-inning rally to beat the

Red Sox 5–3 and win the American League pennant by a single game.

The 1949 World Series was another Subway Series, with the Yankees pitted against the Brooklyn Dodgers, who had won the National League by a single game. History was made when game five was completed under the artificial lights at Ebbets Field, the first time lights had been used in the World Series; that game saw the Yankees win 4–1 over their neighbors. Casey Stengel had won the biggest prize in baseball in his first attempt, and his success story did not finish there. He would write himself into the record books as the only man to manage a team to five consecutive World Series titles.

BELOW LEFT: Casey Stengel standing on the field before a 1956 World Series game at Ebbets Field.

BELOW: Charles Dillon Stengel, holding court at a press conference in January 1954. Would they win a sixth straight World Series in 1954? As it happened, the answer was no.

Yogi Berra

Although he played, coached, and managed the New York Mets during his career, it was in his time with the New York Yankees—in all three capacities—that Yogi Berra made his name.

Born Lawrence Peter Berra in St. Louis, Missouri, on May 12, 1925, he was known as "Lawdie" as a child (due to the inability of his Italian mother to pronounce his given name properly). He reputedly got the nickname "Yogi" for always sitting cross-legged, like an Indian yogi.

After dropping out of school in the eighth grade, Berra was playing baseball in the local American Legion when he was spotted by the St. Louis Cardinals. The Cardinals had just signed Yogi's friend Joe Garagiola for $500 but offered Yogi just $250, which Yogi duly turned down. According to legend, the Cardinals were not too bothered by the refusal, believing they had signed the better prospect and supposedly claiming that Berra would "never make anything more than a Triple A ballplayer at best." Fortunately, Yankees scout Leo Browne disagreed, also believing that Berra was worth the $500 he was holding out for, and signed him in 1942.

Initially assigned to the Norfolk Tars of the Class B Piedmont League, Berra volunteered for the U.S. Navy when he turned 18 in 1943, and took part in the D-Day landings at Normandy in 1944. After the war he was sent to the New London team in Connecticut. It was while playing for New London that Berra's stock began to rise, for Mel Ott of the New York Giants saw him play and called the Yankees to offer $50,000 for his contract. The Yankees' general manager, Larry MacPhail, had no idea who Berra was, but reasoned that if the Giants valued him at $50,000 he had to be something special. MacPhail turned the offer down and recalled Berra, sending him to the Newark Bears for a brief spell to complete his transition into a professional ballplayer. Berra made his debut at Yankee Stadium in 1946 as a platoon catcher with Aaron Robinson, Charlie Silvera, and Gus Niarhos.

both Berra and Bill Dickey, his predecessor as the Yankees' catcher. Berra was not only a star catcher, he was (and still is) a larger-than-life character, as well known for his comments off the field as for his accomplishments on it.

Indeed, his "Yogi-isms" are so well known it would be impossible to select the best. He coined the phrase "It ain't over till it's over," and once gave the sage advice "Always go to other people's funerals, otherwise they won't go to yours."

LEFT: Berra slides in safe at third base as he eludes the attempted tag of Eddie Miksis of the Brooklyn Dodgers on October 8, 1949.

BELOW: Berra in the Yankees' locker room in March 1957, showing off the trademark grin (and ears).

Although known as something of a wild swinger, he was extremely effective and seldom struck out. In 1950 he fanned only 12 times in 597 at bats, making him a tough out for any pitcher.

He played in 15 All-Star Games, won the AL MVP three times (in 1951, 1954, and 1955), and appeared in 14 World Series, of which 10 were won. He was named the Yankees' manager in 1964 and would go on to win the AL pennant in his first season. He was sacked after losing to the Cardinals in the World Series, although it was claimed he would have been dismissed even if he had won the pennant.

Undeterred, Berra picked up his career with the New York Mets, signing as player-coach in 1965 in what was seen as a public-relations coup for the Mets. He retired from the playing side after a single season and concentrated on coaching for the next seven years, eventually taking over as manager in 1972. His best season was 1973, when he lifted the team from last place going into the

final month of the season to win the National League pennant.

He was dismissed in 1975 and returned to the Yankees the following year as a coach. The team would go on to win the AL title in each of the next three seasons, as well as the World Series in 1977 and 1978, with this success fueling his reputation as something of a lucky charm where the Yankees were concerned. Berra was hired as manager before the 1984 season and agreed to continue the following season after being given assurances he would not be fired. Unfortunately, impatience from the owners resulted in his dismissal after the 16th game of the season; the event created a rift that endured for some 15 years.

Berra ended his baseball career as the bench coach of the Houston Astros, joining the team in 1986 and spending three years in the role. He was inducted into the Baseball Hall of Fame in 1972, with the Yankees retiring the number 8 he wore on his uniform the same year in recognition of

YANKEES
THEN AND NOW

BRONX BOMBSHELLS

Female fans have always been attracted to baseball, and the trend is growing

ABOVE: Baseball in the past was a rowdy affair, and women were encouraged to attend games as a civilizing influence. Most clubs promoted ladies' days where women enjoyed discounted ticket prices. These were often for unattractive midweek games, but the Yankees' ladies' days were generally on Saturdays. Here, two elderly fans sit in the stands at Yankee Stadium's very first ladies' day on May 25, 1938.

TOP: Two women on opposing sides of the Dodgers–Yankees rivalry are pictured at Yankee Stadium in 1945.

ABOVE: In the bleachers of Yankee Stadium on June 3, 1945, these Yankee supporters would have to wait a while before the return of Joe DiMaggio and other Yankee players from World War II.

LEFT: An adoring fan dashes out of the stands to get closer to her idol, Mickey Mantle. When the slugger retired from baseball after an 18-year career, the Yankees celebrated June 8, 1969, as Mickey Mantle Day. As part of the festivities, Mantle was driven around the ballpark in a customized buggy—and the temptation proved just too much for some fans.

BELOW LEFT: Morganna Roberts, "the Kissing Bandit," was a familiar sight at MLB stadiums for over two decades. Her quest was to kiss a player in each ballpark. Having vaulted the wall behind home plate, she runs to plant a smacker on Yankees first baseman Don Mattingly during a game against the California Angels on August 25, 1986.

RIGHT: A Yankees fan heads to her seat before a game against the Texas Rangers on August 26, 2002. She is obviously a fan of pitcher Andy Pettitte, who wore number 46.

RIGHT: Derek Jeter fans wave banners before a game against the Chicago White Sox at Yankee Stadium on June 28, 2012. Baseball enjoys the highest percentage of female fans of any of the four major sports in the United States. A Gallup poll in 2012 found that 46 percent of women were fans of the game, and the number is constantly increasing—in 2002, it stood at 37 percent. It has been widely reported in the media that women now comprise up to 47 percent of baseball's total audience. In 2010 the Yankees established a Women's Mini-Fantasy Camp at their base in Tampa, Florida, where women can enjoy a three-day course in baseball, taught by retired pros such as Tino Martinez and Darryl Strawberry.

Phil Rizzuto 10

The name of Phil Rizzuto is familiar to generations of Yankee fans. "The Scooter" made the transition from diamond to commentary booth after retiring as a player in 1956, covering the games for radio and television and amassing a sizable following due to his idiosyncratic style. His oft-imitated catch phrase was "Holy cow!" while his banter with other commentators and vivid play descriptions are the stuff of legend.

Born on September 25, 1917, in Brooklyn, he was rejected by both the New York Giants and the Brooklyn Dodgers due to his lack of height and bulk: he stood just 5 feet 6 inches tall and weighed barely 150 pounds. But a season in the minor leagues with Kansas City, where he posted a .347 average in 1940, persuaded the Yankees that his talent exceeded his stature. They decided to take a chance and were richly rewarded. His major league career, which began in 1941 when he replaced the veteran Frank Crosetti, extended to 1956, with the exception of the war years, and was spent entirely at Yankee Stadium.

As a shortstop, Rizzuto specialized in the double play, for which speed and timing of the throw are essential. Over his career he was involved in 1,217 double plays—at 89 per 1,000 innings, the highest rate in baseball history. He combined with the likes of Joe Gordon, Gerry Priddy, and future commentator Jerry Coleman on second base. Experts rate him the best ever in baseball history. "I hustled and got on base and made the double play," he said. "That's all the Yankees needed in those days."

At the plate, he had speed, stealth, and was a master bunter. His best season came in 1950, when he hit .324 and scored 125 runs; the MVP Award was well deserved, as he had been the runner-up the previous season.

His stats weren't enough on their own to win him an automatic place in the Baseball Hall of Fame, but he made it anyway in 1994. He was voted in by the Veterans Committee, on which friends like Yogi Berra, Bill White, and Pee Wee Reese then sat, which reconsiders candidates rejected by sportswriters. His inclusion remains a hot topic of debate among baseball critics and fans alike. But Rizzuto said, "I'll take any way to get into the Hall of Fame. If they want a batboy, I'll go in as a batboy."

Along with Joe DiMaggio, Rizzuto played a major role in leading the Yankees back to World Series glory in 1947, after the horrors of wartime. He had served in the U.S. Army for three years and, while it took him time to reestablish his average, he had achieved this by his MVP year. He was a defensive specialist who contributed to the Yankees winning 10 American League pennants and eight World Series championships. Five of the latter triumphs came in consecutive seasons from 1949 to 1953. His Hall of Fame plaque describes him—accurately—as the team's anchor.

Yankees manager Casey Stengel, who rejected him while with the Brooklyn Dodgers, ended up managing Rizzuto during five consecutive championship seasons. He would later say, "He is the greatest shortstop I have ever seen in my entire baseball career, and I have watched some

beauties." Rizzuto's number 10 was retired in a ceremony at Yankee Stadium in August 1985.

"Scooter," as he was universally known, enjoyed his nickname thanks to minor league teammate Billy Hitchcock, who admired Rizzuto's swift baserunning. He spent 40 years as a broadcaster, and became widely recognized and parodied. Singer Meat Loaf even used an excerpt from a Rizzuto broadcast in his 1978 hit song "Paradise by the Dashboard Light."

Phil Rizzuto died in 2007 at the age of 89. His *New York Times* obituary summed him up: "He was a 5-foot-6-inch, 150-pound sparkplug who did the little things right, from turning the pivot on a double play to laying down a perfect sacrifice bunt. He left the slugging to powerful teammates like Joe DiMaggio, Mickey Mantle, Tommy Henrich, Charlie Keeler, and Yogi Berra."

LEFT: No glove required: Rizzuto holds up a foul ball he caught in the Yankee Stadium press box during a game between the Yankees and the Washington Senators in May 1960.

ABOVE: Rizzuto was popular with the fans long before his 40-year broadcasting career gave the sport phrases like "Holy cow!" and "You huckleberry!"

STADIUM SCOREBOARD

The Yankees always wanted the biggest and the best

ABOVE: When Yankee Stadium opened in 1923, the original manually operated scoreboard was situated behind the right-field bleachers. It was large enough to be visible to spectators in all parts of the stadium. In 1937, when improvements were made to the stadium, a new scoreboard was installed. It was 150 feet high with an Art Deco Longines clock positioned on top. The scoreboard also contained ten speakers for broadcasting announcements.

This was replaced by a brand-new, partly electronic version in 1946, a real innovation at the time that was hailed as "the most efficient scoreboard ever built and, in general, a big stride forward." It was operated by just two men as opposed to five for the previous model. Among its features were a glare-free enamel covering and a new Longines clock. In this picture it shows the score during game four of the World Series between the Brooklyn Dodgers and the Yankees on October 7, 1956. When a new scoreboard debuted at the start of the 1959 season, the *New York Times* hailed it as "the electronic miracle." This was Major League Baseball's first all-electronic scoreboard, and also the first to display messages. It stood 35 feet high and 73 feet long. Around 115,000 watts

ulsed through a structure that weighed 25 tons. Its letters and numbers were up to 24 feet tall. Details of out-of-town games were displayed on a separate bank. The "electronic marvel" lasted until September 30, 1973, the last game at the stadium prior to its refurbishment, when the final message read, "Thanks for the memories, see you all there in 1976!" One of the most poignant messages was flashed on the replacement screen on August 3, 1979. "Our captain and our leader has not left us—today, tomorrow, this year, next . . . our endavors will reflect our love and admiration for him."

ABOVE: The new stadium has continued the tradition of innovation with a scoreboard capable of showing video replays and action from other games, much to the consternation of baseball's governing body. Pictured in Septembe 2012, the new Yankee Stadium's high-definition scoreboard is a marvel. Six times larger than its predecessor, the Mitsubishi Diamond Vision LED video board measures 103 feet by 59 feet. It is flanked by two smaller screens, the one on the right displaying advertisements while the other functions as, among other things, the out-of-town scoreboard.

THE LOCKER ROOM

Donning the pinstripes has never been so comfortable

ABOVE: Manager Casey Stengel addresses his team during spring training in 1949 at Miller Huggins Park in St. Petersburg, Florida. Previously known as Crescent Park, the facility was renamed after the Yankees' chief when he died suddenly in 1929. Although only a training facility, the locker room wasn't far removed from the kind the team would use through the course of the regular season. The wood-burning stove was their only luxury.

RIGHT: One of the most poignant locker room shots was taken on Sunday June 13, 1948, as Babe Ruth prepared for his final appearance in pinstripes. Fifty thousand fans filled Yankee Stadium for a game against the Cleveland Indians. They had also come to pay tribute to Babe Ruth whose No. 3 was being retired. Throat cancer had taken its toll on the great man and he was given a bat to steady himself as he walked slowly onto the field to take the waves of applause. He died two months later at the age of 53.

RIGHT: The carpeted luxury of the home team's locker room photographed prior to the opening of the new Yankee Stadium in 2009.

ABOVE: Slugger Reggie Jackson answers reporters' questions in the Yankee Stadium dressing room after his team's victory over the Cleveland Indians on September 30, 1978, shortly after a legal challenge that forced a change in policy on postgame interviews. In 1975 Major League Baseball commissioner Bowie Kuhn banned female sportswriters from locker rooms on the grounds of decency. The case came to court in 1978, and the policy was deemed unconstitutional under the equal opportunities law. As a response, the Yankees allowed the press to enter the locker room for 15 minutes following a game, after which the doors were closed for 45 minutes while the players dressed.

LEFT: The preserved locker of former team captain Thurman Munson at Yankee Stadium in 2008. The locker had been kept empty after Munson's death in a plane crash in August 1979. When the Yankees moved to the new stadium in 2009, the locker was moved to the museum there.

★ **If the Yankees were a major force in baseball** throughout much of the 1930s and 1940s, then the following decade saw them truly become the dominant team. They reached the World Series every year except two, and added another five World Series pennants to their record. This success was achieved with much coming and going on and off the field, proof that in baseball nothing ever stands still. The chief departure had

been Joe DiMaggio, whose retirement was imminent for a couple of years. DiMaggio had made little secret of wishing to bow out at the very top with his reputation intact, before he became just an "ordinary player." For any other player, suffering a bone spur would have been considered a minor injury, but in Joe DiMaggio's case it presented the perfect way for him to exit the game. Just as the fans and team bade farewell to

the Yankee Clipper, others were ready to step into his shoes, with Mickey Mantle in particular adding his name to the roll call of Yankee greats. The Yankees extended their World Series run with victories over the Philadelphia Phillies in 1950 and the New York Giants in 1951 before locking horns with the Brooklyn Dodgers in 1952 and 1953. The first was another close-run affair, the Yankees emerging 4–3 victors, and the following year's battle was nearly as close, with the Yankees winning in six games. Collective success for the Yankees was achieved thanks to individual players turning in star performances. Phil Rizzuto was named MVP in 1950, followed a year later by Yogi Berra. Gil McDougald was named Rookie of the Year in 1951, the first Yankee to attain the honor, on the back of a .306 batting average, 14 home runs, and 63 runs batted in.

Although there was to be recognition for Yogi Berra (MVP) and Bob Grim (Rookie of the Year) in 1954, the team finished second in the American League, their first season without a title since 1948. The pennant was recaptured the following year (as was Berra's MVP Award, making him the first Yankees player to retain the award; it was the third of his career), although the World Series was lost to the Brooklyn Dodgers in seven games. The following year saw a repeat, with the Yankees this time prevailing in seven games. Mickey Mantle was named American League MVP, while Don Larsen was named the World Series MVP after throwing the only perfect game in World Series history. Elston Howard also secured his place in Yankees history in 1955, when he became the first African American player in team history. Howard made an immediate impact, getting a hit in his first at bat, and would go on to give the Yankees 11 seasons before winding down his career with the Boston Red Sox.

While the Yankees lost the World Series in 1957, being beaten by the Milwaukee Braves 4–3, the major talking point of the year was the departure of both the Dodgers and Giants for California. The dual move left the Yankees as the city's only team, although they had long previously attained the status of the city's best; battles with the Giants

and Dodgers would be resumed in the following decade. That World Series loss in 1957 came despite Mickey Mantle being named league MVP for the second consecutive season and stretching the Yankees' ownership of the award to four straight seasons. Twenty-year-old Tony Kubek was named Rookie of the Year, just reward for his performance in the World Series, in which he hit two home runs, scored three times, and drove in four runs.

A year later the Yankees got their revenge, winning the American League pennant and then overcoming the Braves by the same 4–3 score; the Yankees became only the second team to win the series after being down three games to one. Bob Turley won the Cy Young Award, and was named the World Series MVP.

After four straight American League pennants, the Yankees ended the decade empty-handed, finishing in third place behind the Chicago White Sox and the Cleveland Indians, their worst finish since 1948.

ABOVE: On October 8, 1956, Don Larsen pitched his World Series perfect game; Yogi Berra leaping into Larsen's arms after the final out is one of baseball's most memorable images.

LEFT: Members of the New York Yankees and Brooklyn Dodgers line up to greet President Dwight D. Eisenhower on the opening day of the 1956 World Series.

RIGHT: Phil Rizzuto at spring training in Florida in 1953.

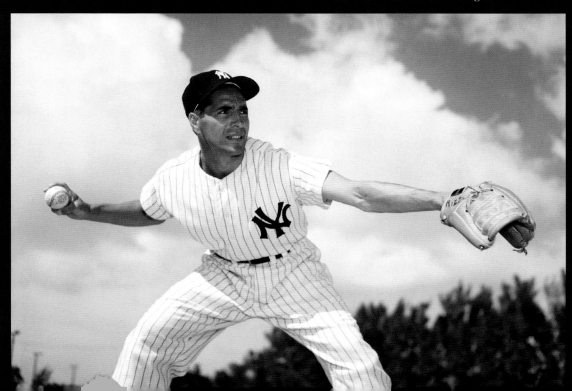

MICKEY MANTLE MAKES HIS MAJOR LEAGUE DEBUT AGAINST BOSTON

ABOVE: Casey Stengel seems to be giving Mickey Mantle some advice as they confer over the bat rack at Cleveland Municipal Stadium before the game against the Cleveland Indians on August 25, 1951.

Six months shy of his twentieth birthday, Mickey Mantle strode onto the field at Yankee Stadium to make his major league debut in front of an expectant crowd of 44,860. The 19-year-old was already feted as an outstanding prospect; the press had labeled him the "new Babe Ruth" and he was to play right field, in Ruth's old position. Mantle also was seen as the natural heir to Joe DiMaggio, and the torch would pass to the youngster at the end of the year when DiMaggio announced his retirement.

After spring training, Yankees manager Casey Stengel commented, "I never saw a player who had greater promise. That young fellow has me terribly confused. He should have a year in Triple A ball, but with his combination of speed and power he should win the triple batting crown every year. In fact, he should do anything he wants to do."

Mantle's debut was originally scheduled for a three-game series on the road at Washington, but rain put an end to those plans. He had taken part in the Yankees' spring training in Phoenix, where his performances were so impressive that Stengel decided to give him his major league debut rather than farm him out to the minors. During the team's preseason tour of the West Coast, Mantle hit a massive 550-foot home run at the University of Southern California.

Before the start of the 1951 season, Mantle was called to a draft board hearing in Kansas City. Having contracted the bone infection osteomyelitis in his leg while playing college football, he had been ruled unfit for service, but the controversy over how he could still be fit to play baseball dogged his early career. Classified as medically exempt again, he flew back to New York to play in two exhibition games against the Brooklyn Dodgers at Ebbets Field. Mickey went 4 for 4 in the second game.

His debut came on April 17, 1951, and the Yankees recorded a 5–0 win over the Red Sox. Wearing number 6, Mantle batted third after Jackie Jensen and Phil Rizzuto, with DiMaggio fourth. In his first at bat against Boston's Bill Wight, Mantle grounded out to second base. His second attempt, he popped up to third. During the sixth inning, he hit a single off Wight to drive in Rizzuto for the third run of the game. Mantle advanced to second on a DiMaggio hit and was driven in on a hit by Yogi Berra. He ended the afternoon 1 for 4 with an RBI, the first of a career total of 1,509 RBIs. The Yankees won the game 5–0 behind pitcher Vic Raschi.

As the first month of the season progressed, Mantle struggled to adjust to major league pitching. The weight of expectations was starting to affect his game. He was sent to the Yankees' minor league team, the Kansas City Blues, where his form continued to suffer through an 0-for-21 slump. On the verge of quitting, he managed to turn things around and returned to the Yankees to play in two games of the World Series against the Dodgers.

LEFT: Mantle's first World Series ended early after he caught his spikes in a grating while chasing a fly ball from Willie Mays in center field, wrenching his knee.

BELOW: Two of the greats with a future great. DiMaggio and Boston's Ted Williams pose with the young Mantle in 1951.

ABOVE: Babe Ruth shakes hands with President Warren Harding at Yankee Stadium on April 24, 1923.

BELOW: Record-chasers Mickey Mantle (right) and Roger Maris (left) pose with President Harry S. Truman before the start of a doubleheader with the Washington Senators on September 4, 1961.

YANKEES AND THE PRESIDENTS

Presidents of the United States are no strangers to Yankee games

ABOVE: William H. Taft set a precedent as the first U.S. president to throw a ceremonial first pitch at a baseball game in April 1910. Here he performs the service for the Yankees at Hilltop Park in July of that same year.

FAR RIGHT: Bill Clinton poses with a New York Yankees uniform presented by pitcher Orlando Hernandez during a visit to the White House by the Yankees' 1998 World Series–winning team on June 10, 1999.

RIGHT: Dwight D. Eisenhower throws out the ceremonial first pitch from the stands at Griffith Stadium on the opening day of the 1956 season. Yankees manager Casey Stengel looks on. The pair would meet up at the end of the season at Ebbets Field, when the Dodgers and Yankees were introduced to the president before the start of the World Series.

BELOW: President Barack Obama is presented with an autographed New York Yankees jersey by manager Joe Girardi during the traditional White House visit by the World Series champions on April 26, 2010.

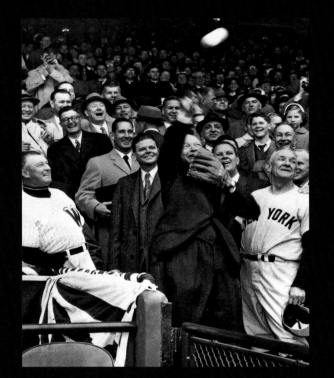

A CAPITAL GAME

Ever since Abraham Lincoln had a baseball field constructed behind the White House, presidents of the United States have been closely associated with the national pastime. Visits by the World Series champions to the White House and presidents' first pitches in Washington are woven into the fabric of the game. George H. W. Bush played first base at Yale University; his son George W. Bush co-owned the Texas Rangers from 1989 to 1998. In 1988 Ronald Reagan memorably provided play-by-play commentary of a game between the Chicago Cubs and the Pittsburgh Pirates. Franklin D. Roosevelt deemed baseball so important to national morale that it continued to be played during World War II. The game has helped many presidents show a connection to everyday fans, but they must be careful to maintain at least a show of neutrality. Barack Obama learned this lesson in Boston when, during a 2012 speech, he tried to joke about the trade of a player from the Red Sox to his favorite team, the Chicago White Sox, and was drowned out by a chorus of boos.

THE YANKEES WIN A FIFTH STRAIGHT WORLD SERIES

ABOVE: Billy Martin is mobbed by his teammates after singling home the run that ended the game and clinched the 1953 World Series.

The 1953 World Series was the third straight all-New York affair; the Giants had lost to the Yankees in 1951, and this was a rematch of the previous year's Subway Series between the Brooklyn Dodgers and the Yankees. The Dodgers were eager to avenge their 4–3 defeat of 1952 while the Yankees were on the verge of bettering their own record of four straight world titles from 1936 to 1939.

In the regular season, the Bronx Bombers claimed the division title with a record of 99–52, winning their 20th pennant, finishing 8½ games ahead of the Cleveland Indians. In the National League, the Dodgers had been equally dominant.

The first two games were played at Yankee Stadium, where the home team took the opening games 9–5 and 4–2. Mickey Mantle's two-out, two-run homer proved decisive in the second game. Brooklyn evened the series by winning the next two games at Ebbets Field. Game three saw the Dodgers' Carl Erskine set a new World Series record when he struck out 14 Yankee batters.

The turning point came in the third inning of game five in Brooklyn. The Yankees were leading 2–1 when Mantle powered a grand slam into the upper deck of left field, putting the Yankees ahead by the score 6–1. The final score was 11–7, and the two teams headed back to Yankee Stadium for the sixth game.

Brooklyn was down 3–1 but came back to tie the game in the top of the ninth inning, before the Yankees took their turn at bat. Second baseman Billy Martin was the hero of the hour, driving in the winning run with a single to center. It was the fifth time that the Dodgers had lost to the Yankees in the World Series, although they finally got some measure of revenge in 1955.

The history books were rewritten again with an unprecedented fifth consecutive world title for manager Casey Stengel and the Yankees. It remains an unsurpassed achievement. The Bronx Bombers would win three straight World Series from 1998 to 2000. The only other team to match that feat was the Oakland A's from 1972 to 1974.

BELOW LEFT: Dodgers fans prepare for the first game of the 1953 World Series at Yankee Stadium equipped with their own homemade megaphones. The Yankees won the game 9–5.

BELOW: The original caption from September 30, 1953, reads: "The powerhouse of the Yankees' 9–5 victory over the Brooklyn Dodgers in the 1953 series opener pose happily in the Yanks' dressing room after the game. From left to right are: Hank Bauer, who accounted for a triple; Yogi Berra, who scored one of the game's homers; Billy Martin, who smashed a three-run triple; and Joe Collins, who belted a homer."

Whitey Ford 16

Whitey Ford holds a special place of affection among Yankee fans, spending his entire 16-year career pitching for the team, racking up a treasure trove of awards and honors. Combine that with the fact that he served his country in the Korean War and you've got a true all-American hero.

He was born Edward Charles Ford in New York on October 21, 1928, just a few miles from what would become his spiritual home, Yankee Stadium. After graduating from Aviation High School in Queens, he was signed by the Yankees as a free agent in 1947 and sent to the minor leagues, where he acquired his nickname of "Whitey" thanks to his blond hair.

He joined the Yankees midway through the 1950 season and made an immediate impact, winning nine straight games before a home run by Sam Chapman of Philadelphia gave him his only loss. In the World Series he was equally effective, pitching 8.2 innings without an earned run to win the fourth game of the Yankee sweep. Ford missed the next two seasons as he served in the U.S. Army, seeing action in the Korean War. Returning to the Yankees in 1953, he picked up where he left off, posting 18–6 and 16–8 records in 1953 and 1954, helping the Yankees to the World Series in 1953. The Yankees already had a "Big Three" pitching staff with Allie Reynolds, Vic Raschi, and Eddie Lopat; the addition of Ford made it the "Big Four."

Although initially the fourth pitcher, Ford would eventually become the ace of the rotation, earning another nickname, "the Chairman of the Board," in recognition of his ability to remain calm during the course of high-pressure games. His 18–7 record in 1955 tied him for the most wins in the AL, and he also led the league in complete games (18) and was second in earned run average (2.63). In the final month of the season he pitched consecutive one-hitters, and the following season

went even better, going 19–6 to lead the team. He would go on to lead the league in ERA for the second time in 1958 with 2.01.

By 1960 Ford found his starts limited, with manager Casey Stengel invariably resting him for at least four days between appearances, usually to ensure his availability against the better teams. The arrival of new manager Ralph Houk in 1961 saw Ford back in a regular four-man rotation, and he responded by posting the most starts in the AL (39) and innings pitched (283), and would win the Cy Young Award with a 25–4 record, leading the major leagues in wins and winning percentage. Two years later, Ford again led the field in wins, winning percentage, starts, and innings pitched with a 24–7 mark.

In 1964 he became a player-coach for the Yankees, a position he retained for the next three seasons until arm problems forced his retirement at the age of 38. By the time he bowed out of playing in 1967, Ford had amassed six World Series victories, appeared in the All-Star Game on ten occasions (missing out only in 1957 and 1963), and had won a total of 11 pennants with the Yankees.

Apart from picking up the Cy Young Award in 1961, Ford had also been named the MVP of the World Series that season as well as collecting the Babe Ruth Award. During the course of his career Ford would register the most World Series wins (10), games started (22), and innings pitched.

Ford was inducted into the National Baseball Hall of Fame in 1974, the same year the Yankees retired his number 16. He was the first Yankee pitcher to have his number retired by the team.

TOP: October 1960: Ford opens the third game of the World Series.

ABOVE: Starting pitchers Warren Spahn of the Milwaukee Braves and Whitey Ford face the cameras at Yankee Stadium before the fourth game of the 1958 World Series.

RIGHT: Yogi Berra embraces rookie pitcher Whitey Ford in the locker room after a doubleheader with the Washington Senators in September 1950.

REMEMBERING THE GREATS

Part of the unique aura that surrounds the Yankees is their embrace and celebration of the past

ABOVE: Yankees owners Dan Topping (left) and Del Webb place floral arrangements at the monuments to Miller Huggins, Lou Gehrig, and Babe Ruth on opening day, April 14, 1953, when the Yankees faced the Philadelphia A's. The first monument erected was that of former manager Huggins after his death in 1929. The freestanding block of red granite, similar to a tombstone, was positioned by the center-field fence and contained a bronze plaque. The tributes to Gehrig and Ruth were added after their deaths. Plaques were later added to the outfield wall. Seen here from the backstop position, the monuments were originally within the field of play and it was unusual for a ball hit on the fly to reach that far. Former Boston Red Sox center fielder Jim Piersall recalls sitting on Babe Ruth's monument during quiet periods of the game. Monument Park was relocated behind the center-field fence during the refurbishment of Yankee Stadium in the mid-1970s.

RIGHT: Monument Park was re-created in the new stadium in 2009. The practice of adding plaques to commemorate retired numbers began in June 1969 with Mickey Mantle. In addition to Huggins, former managers Casey Stengel and Joe McCarthy, along with general manager Ed Barrow, have been honored with plaques but have no uniform numbers to display. A monument is a posthumous honor and, as of 2012 only six people—Miller Huggins, Babe Ruth, Lou Gehrig, Joe DiMaggio, Mickey Mantle, and owner George Steinbrenner—have received this tribute. In recognition of their outstanding contributions to Yankee history, two broadcasters have also been granted plaques. Bob Sheppard served as announcer for more than 4,500 Yankee games over a 56-year period. Mel Allen was known as the "Voice of the Yankees" during his three-decade career as play-by-play commentator.

LEFT AND ABOVE: From left to right in the order they were retired: Gehrig (4), Ruth (3), DiMaggio (5), Mantle (7), Stengel (37), Dickey (8), Berra (8), Ford (16), Munson (15), Howard (32), Maris (9), Rizzuto (10), Martin (1), Jackson (44), Mattingly (23), Guidry (49), and Jackie Robinson, whose number 42 was retired throughout baseball in 1997.

BELOW: The first monument to be erected was for Yankees manager Miller Huggins (center), who died at the age of 50.

GAME CHANGERS
KEY MOMENTS IN YANKEE HISTORY

DON LARSEN THROWS THE ONLY PERFECT GAME IN WORLD SERIES HISTORY

ABOVE: Larsen pitches to Junior Gilliam, the Dodgers' leadoff hitter.

The perfect game—27 up, 27 down—is one of the rarest feats in baseball; as of 2012, it has been achieved only 23 times in major league history. Don Larsen's 1956 perfect game remains the only one thrown in the World Series. It was the fourth in the modern era (which began in 1900) and the first in 34 years. The feat earned him the World Series Most Valuable Player Award and the Babe Ruth Award for the best postseason performance.

Larsen was born on August 7, 1929, in Michigan City, Indiana. He established a reputation for baseball while in the army and signed for the St. Louis Browns on leaving the service, making his major league debut in 1953. The Browns relocated to Baltimore in 1954, and Larsen was traded to New York in 1955. Manager Casey Stengel used him as a backup starter and occasional reliever. He had a reputation as a guy who loved the nightlife.

In 1955, after a poor start to the season, he was sent to the minors, and played for the Denver Bears for most of the season. After being recalled to the Bronx in 1956, his form improved and it proved to be his best season; he achieved an 11–5 record, 107 strikeouts, and a 3.26 ERA. He started 20 games and relieved in 18 others. Toward the end of the season, he adopted an unorthodox delivery that lacked a windup.

The 1956 World Series matchup with the Dodgers was a repeat of the previous year's. Larsen's first start came in game two at Ebbets Field, and it was not auspicious. He gave up only one hit but walked four Dodgers for four runs as the Yankees squandered a 6–0 lead and lost the game 13–8 to fall two games behind in the series. The Yankees rallied, winning the next two games at Yankee Stadium. Larsen feared that he would not be called on to pitch again, but was unexpectedly named to start game five at Yankee Stadium. Manager Casey Stengel told him the news only a few hours before the start. Larsen said, "When it was over, I was so happy, I felt like crying. I wanted to win this one for Casey. After what I did in Brooklyn, he could have forgotten about me

and who would blame him? But he gave me another chance and I'm grateful."

The crowd of 64,519 cheered him on as he retired 27 Dodgers. On the way to the perfect game, he was helped by three terrific fielding plays. The most memorable of these came in the fifth inning when Gil Hodges hit a line drive toward Death Valley, but Mickey Mantle made a stunning leaping catch. Larsen's no-windup style paid dividends as he dismissed a team with a .604 winning percentage, the highest ever to concede a perfect game. Only one Dodgers batter, Pee Wee Reese, worked a three-ball count.

On his 97th pitch, Larsen struck out pinch-hitter Dale Mitchell to complete the gem. The image of catcher Yogi Berra leaping into Larsen's arms at the end of the game has become one of baseball's most iconic. The Yankees won 2–0 and took the series 4–3.

BELOW AND BELOW LEFT: Larsen threw them and Berra caught them. The Yankees pitcher became an instant celebrity and did various promotional appearances, including a guest spot on Bob Hope's TV show. He was traded to the Kansas City A's in 1961 and went on to play for the Chicago White Sox, San Francisco Giants, Houston Colt .45s, Baltimore Orioles, and Chicago Cubs. The perfect game was Larsen's greatest moment; as he proudly stated, "They can never break my record. The best they can do is tie it."

Mickey Mantle

It was preordained that Mickey Mantle was going to become a professional baseball player; his father named him after the Philadelphia Athletics' Mickey Cochrane. While it might have appeared to be a daunting task to try and emulate the exploits and accomplishments of the Hall of Fame catcher, history has shown that Mickey Mantle surpassed him.

Although Mickey Charles Mantle was born in Spavinaw, Oklahoma, on October 20, 1930, the family soon moved across the state to Commerce, where his father, Mutt, worked in the lead and zinc mines. Each day after work he would take Mickey out to some land next to an old tin barn in order to practice baseball, pitching tennis balls right-handed to Mickey to bat left-handed. Then his grandfather Charlie would enter the fray, pitching left-handed for Mickey to bat right-handed. By the age of 10, "the Mick" was already considered a prospect.

Mantle had already experienced minor league baseball by the time he attended Commerce High School. A serious shin injury, sustained while playing football in 1946, threatened his sports career, for he developed osteomyelitis in the bone, which could have resulted in amputation. Fortunately, the injury responded to treatment with penicillin, although the condition would remain a nagging reminder for the duration of his career.

In 1948 Mantle was playing semiprofessional baseball for the Baxter Springs Whizz Kids when he was spotted by a Yankee scout. That scout would return to Commerce on the day Mantle graduated from high school, and secured his signature on a professional contract for $140 a month and a $1,150 signing bonus. Initially dispatched to the Class D Independence Yankees, he fell out of love with baseball altogether. In a telephone call home, Mantle expressed his intention of quitting the game. Mutt drove

over to Independence and convinced his son that professional baseball was a much better life than working in the mines.

After moving up a league in 1950, Mantle was invited along to the Yankees' instructional camp in Phoenix, Arizona, in 1951. Although the Yankees intended to let him play the 1951 season in the minors, his performance at the spring camp gained him a place in the majors, and he was assigned the number 6. The number created pressure, as it indicated that the Yankees considered Mantle the next in line for greatness after Ruth (3), Gehrig (4), and DiMaggio (5).

After an impressive start, Mantle entered a slump and was sent to the Kansas City Blues to try to restore his confidence. Again Mantle called his father and told him he wanted to quit. Mutt

traveled to Kansas and gave him the required pep talk. Mantle then broke out of his slump and was recalled to the Yankees, this time being given the number 7 uniform.

He moved to center field in 1952, replacing DiMaggio. Over the next 16 years he would help the Yankees win seven World Series, earn selection for the All-Star Game on 20 occasions, pick up three AL MVP Awards (1956, 1957, and 1962) and win the Gold Glove Award in 1962. His greatest year was undoubtedly 1956, when he led the major leagues with a .353 batting average, 52 home runs, and 130 RBIs. In game five of the World Series that year, Mantle homered and made a spectacular catch to save Don Larsen's historic perfect game.

During the course of the 12 World Series he appeared in, Mantle would register the record for the most home runs with 18. He officially retired in 1969, with the Yankees retiring his number 7, and was inducted into the Hall of Fame in 1974. His career totals include 536 home runs and 2,415 hits, and he batted over .300 in ten seasons, with a top mark of .365 in 1957.

A series of poor business investments threatened his financial position after his career came to an end, but the sudden explosion in the sports memorabilia industry restored his wealth, due in large part to his popularity and items relating to his career. He later moved to Dallas, Texas, where he died on August 13, 1995.

ABOVE LEFT: Mantle with fellow slugger Joe DiMaggio in 1951, Mantle's first season and DiMaggio's last.

LEFT: Mantle slugs another one: the length of the titanic home run he hit against the Senators' Chuck Stobbs in 1953, which flew out of Griffith Stadium, is still debated by baseball fans.

★ **Viewed in isolation, the 1960s were only**
moderately successful for the New York Yankees,
with five appearances in the World Series yielding
just two victories. The problem was that the
Yankees were never viewed in isolation, and even
that record paled in comparison to their exploits
over the previous three decades.

A record of 97 wins in 1960 was enough to claim
the American League, but following their loss to

the Pittsburgh Pirates in seven games, the
Yankees decided it was time to change managers.
It was felt that Stengel was now too old to manage
in the American League, a move that led him to
comment that he had been fired for turning 70,
and he would "never make that mistake again."
After a two-year hiatus, he returned to the game as
manager of the New York Mets, spending a final
four years providing newspaper reporters with
plenty of copy even if his team couldn't do the

business for him on the field. The Yankees hired
Ralph Houk as Stengel's replacement.

Well known around Yankee Stadium, where he
had been a player from 1947 to 1954, Houk had
coached in Denver before returning to the
Yankees as a first-base coach in 1958. In 1960
Houk had taken temporary charge of the Yankees
from late May to early June while Stengel was
sidelined by an illness and, although the team lost

the World Series, the owners saw enough in Houk to suggest he might make a good manager. And so he did, although his volatile temper and confrontational style with umpires (typified by the photo at bottom right) ensured there was never a dull moment. In 1961 his team was virtually unbeatable, led by Roger Maris (who hit a then-record 61 home runs) and Mickey Mantle (54 homers). After winning 109 games in the regular season, they beat the Cincinnati Reds in five games in the World Series. Maris was named the American League MVP, and Whitey Ford, who racked up 25 victories, picked up the Cy Young Award and World Series MVP.

A year later the Yankees were back, their 96 victories earning them a World Series berth against the San Francisco Giants (who, of course, had previously been a New York franchise). The Yankees prevailed in seven games, and Mickey Mantle claimed his third league MVP Award. Tom Tresh won the Rookie of the Year Award, and Ralph Terry was named the World Series MVP. Houk just missed out on three World Series in a row in 1963: after winning 104 games in the regular season, the Yankees were swept by the Dodgers in the World Series. Houk was made general manager after that defeat, with Yogi Berra taking over as manager—but while Berra had achieved legendary status as a player, his managerial qualities were not quite as apparent. Although the Yankees won the American League in 1964, the World Series was lost to the St. Louis Cardinals in seven games. Berra was replaced by Johnny Keane, previously the manager of the Cardinals.

The Yankees that Johnny Keane took control of in 1965 was not the team of the last two-plus decades. Much of the team's roster was getting on in years. There were changes all across the club, with Dan Topping and Del Webb selling 80 percent of their stake in the team to CBS for $11.2 million in 1964. While the purchase was initially seen as being beneficial to the Yankees—for CBS possessed far deeper pockets than the previous owners—the draft system now in place meant the Yankees could no longer outbid other teams for any player they wanted.

The decline was sudden and total; the Yankees plunged to the bottom of the league, the first time since 1912 they finished in the cellar. Keane was fired, and Ralph Houk took over for his second stint as manager, but probably far more alarming for the owners was the sight of just 413 fans rattling around in a stadium that could hold 67,000 for a September 1966 home game against the White Sox.

From the bottom of the league in 1966, the only way for the Yankees was up, and the following year they finished next to last. Getting back to the upper echelons was going to take time, patience, and a new roster. The decade would end with two fifth-place finishes, although they managed to win 83 and 80 games in 1968 and 1969, respectively, well adrift of the figures they had posted at the start of the decade. Mickey Mantle announced his retirement in 1969—a notable point in Yankee history that closed a disappointing decade.

ABOVE: Mel Stottlemyre pitches in front of a sparse crowd at Yankee Stadium in 1968.

FAR LEFT: Roger Maris coasts in after hitting his 61st homer off Red Sox pitcher Tracy Stallard.

LEFT: The heavy-hitting 1960s trinity of Roger Maris, Mickey Mantle, and Elston Howard.

ROGER MARIS HITS 61 HOME RUNS

The 1961 Major League Baseball season saw the American League expand from eight to ten teams, a move followed by the National League in 1962. Accordingly, the schedule was increased from 154 games to 162. The Yankees fielded a team that vies with the lineups of 1927 and 1998 as a candidate for the greatest ever.

At the heart of the team, the big-hitting Mickey Mantle and Roger Maris attracted the attention of the headline writers as they both made a serious assault on Babe Ruth's single-season record of 60 home runs. In 1960, Maris's first season with the Yankees, he was limited by injuries and totaled 39 homers to Mantle's 40. The eight extra games were likely to have an impact on the record, although when asked in January, Maris was dismissive. "Nobody will touch it . . . Look up the records and you'll see that it's a rare year when anybody hits 50 homers, let alone 60." Later in the season, he changed his mind, saying, "I'm not trying to be Babe Ruth; I'm trying to hit 61 home runs and be Roger Maris."

Maris began the season slowly with just one home run to his name in April. He gained momentum in May with 11 home runs, and he hit another 15 in June. With Maris batting third and Mantle fourth, the lead exchanged hands between the two several times during the summer. Maris passed an important milestone when he became the first player to hit 50 home runs by the end of August. Mantle was just behind with 46 when he was sidelined in September by an injured hip. He finished with a career-best 54 homers. Between them, the two sluggers established the home-run

ABOVE: Roger Maris displays the ball caught in the stands by 19-year-old Sal Durante (see page 106).

record for teammates at 115. Dubbed the "M&M Boys," the two were the subject of intense media focus as it became apparent that Ruth's record was under serious threat. Much of the coverage of Maris was negative. The New York newspapers invented a rivalry between him and Mantle when, in reality, they were good friends. Maris's bluntness and lack of savvy in dealing with journalists often worked against him.

Many inside the game were protective of Babe Ruth's record, especially since two more teams had been added to the league and the schedule expanded. In mid-July, baseball commissioner Ford Frick, a friend of Ruth's, announced that the total would have to be surpassed in 154 games or it would go into the record books as a separate record. After 154 games, Maris had 59 home runs.

Maris equaled Ruth's total against the Orioles and, going into the final day of the regular season, needed one more homer to break the 34-year-old record. The Yankees faced the Boston Red Sox in front of a crowd of 23,154 on October 1, 1961.

In the fourth inning, he was at bat facing Boston's Tracy Stallard. The bases were empty and the Yankees had one out. Maris let two pitches go, and then swung hard at a waist-high fastball. It sailed over the right-field wall for the record-breaking 61st home run. Maris rounded the bases, tipped his hat to the crowd, and took four bows before returning to the bench. It was his only career hit off Stallard. The Yankees won the game 1–0 and became world champions again on October 9. Leading the league in home runs and RBIs, Maris was named the Most Valuable Player for the second consecutive year.

However, in 1980 Maris was still bitter about how he had been treated during his record-breaking season, commenting, "They acted as though I was doing something wrong, poisoning the record books or something. Do you know what I have to show for 61 home runs? Nothing. Exactly nothing."

BELOW LEFT: Roger Maris is presented with the 1961 American League Most Valuable Player Award by American League president Joe Cronin prior to a game at Yankee Stadium in 1962.

BELOW: Fifty years later, the family of Roger Maris (who died in 1985 of Hodgkin's lymphoma) visits the new Yankee Stadium for a celebration of the famous 61st home run.

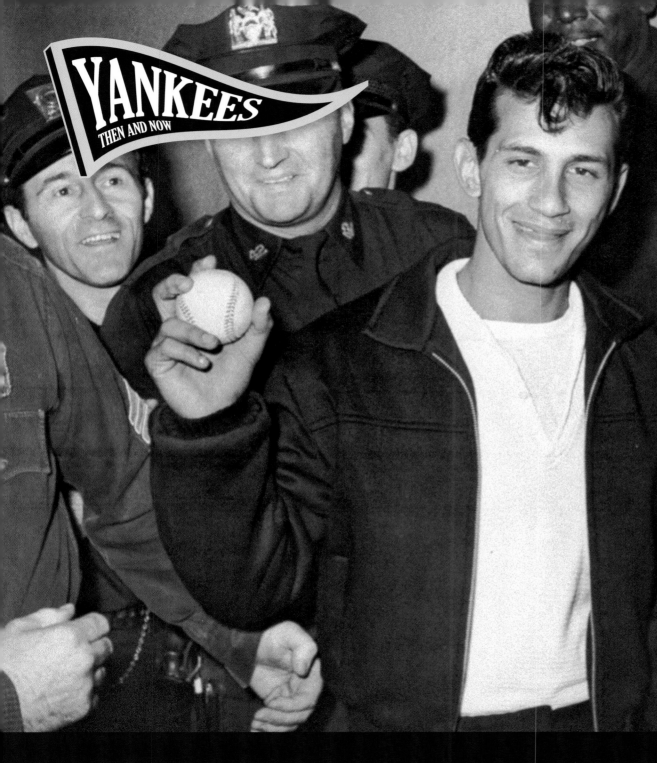

LEFT: At Yankee Stadium on October 1, 1961, Roger Maris hit his 61st home run of the season off a pitch from Tracy Stallard of the Boston Red Sox. The Yankees won 2–0 and the game has gone down in history as the occasion when Maris overtook Babe Ruth's home run record. The lucky fan standing with Maris in the locker room is 19-year-old Sal Durante, who caught the ball that had traveled over 360 feet from home plate to the right-field stands. Durante had only decided to go to the game at the last minute, and was surprised to get tickets so late. Just before Maris's homer, he'd changed seats with his girlfriend to sit in the row behind. "I zoomed in on the ball going to the bat. Next thing I know, I jumped out of my seat and reached as high as I could possibly reach and caught the ball in my right hand."

BELOW: Enjoying his first 15 minutes of fame, Sal Durante proudly displays the home run ball as he poses with Maris in the locker room after the game.

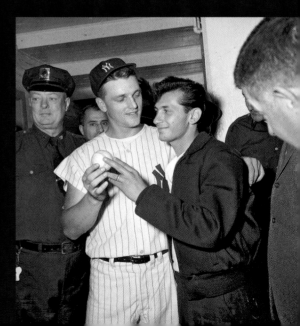

HISTORIC CATCHES

Sal Durante got his 15 minutes of fame in 1961, and then, 50 years later

ABOVE: Fifty years later, in 2011, Sal Durante returned to the new Yankee Stadium and was reunited with the ball he caught in right field all those years ago. He was given his own tour of the stadium. This time, Durante needed a glove for the ball that is now part of Yankee history.

FAMOUS FAN CATCHES

In 1996 during the first game of the American League Championship Series against the Baltimore Orioles, Derek Jeter hit a long drive to right field. As the Orioles' outfielder leaped to try to catch the ball, a 12-year-old fan named Jeffrey Maier stuck his glove out over the fence and caught it. The umpire called a home run instead of fan interference. The Yankees won the game, went on to beat the Orioles, and eventually took the World Series; Jeffrey Maier became a legend.

LEFT: Yankees fan Christian Lopez shakes the hand of Derek Jeter on July 9, 2011, at Yankee Stadium after catching the 3,000th hit of Jeter's career, a home run.

Roger Maris 9

The name of Roger Maris rightly appears in the record books attached to his 1961 eclipse of Babe Ruth's 60 home runs in a season.

Roger Maras was born to a family of Croatian descent in Minnesota on September 10, 1934, and subsequently changed the spelling of his surname to Maris. His imposing physique suggested a future in college football, but he left the University of Oklahoma to sign a $15,000 contract to play baseball for the Cleveland Indians. After four years in the minors, he made his major league debut in 1957 for the Indians. He was traded the following year to the Kansas City Athletics, and was elected to the 1959 All-Star Game. In December 1959 Maris joined the Yankees as part of a trade involving seven players.

His impact was immediate, with the Yankees winning the American League pennant in his first season. He led the league in slugging percentage, runs batted in, and extra-base hits, and was only headed by teammate Mickey Mantle in home runs and total bases. This was achieved despite an injury that caused him to miss 17 games. His defensive skills in the outfield earned him a Gold Glove Award, and he was also declared the American League's Most Valuable Player.

The following season saw Maris hit his record 61 home runs. The Yankees won the World Series and Maris was voted Most Valuable Player in the American League for the second straight year, as he led the league in home runs and RBIs. He was also named the Associated Press's Male Athlete of the Year.

Maris hit 33 home runs in 1962, producing a total of 133 homers since 1960, the most of any player over that span. He also drove in 100 runs for the third straight year and was selected to the All-Star Game for the fourth straight year. The Yankees retained the World Series.

But things went downhill from then on; physical doubts dogged him after he missed almost half the 1963 season,

playing in only 90 games. In 1964 Maris hit 26 home runs and added 71 RBIs, and the Yankees again won the pennant and a trip to the World Series. But a wrist injury restricted him to only 46 games in 1965.

Maris left the Yankees for the St. Louis Cardinals at the end of the 1966 season, helping them to a World Series win the following year and retiring in 1968 after claiming a second pennant in two seasons. Maris played in seven World Series and seven All-Star Games during his career. He hit 275 career home runs and won the 1960 Gold Glove Award for his outstanding defensive play.

Maris's career-defining record stood for 37 years when, in an echo of his own personal battle with Mickey Mantle, it was broken by two men, Mark McGwire and Sammy Sosa. Sadly, Maris himself was not around to see it, having succumbed to cancer in 1985 at the age of 51.

The Yankees retired his number 9 the year before his death, and a plaque in his honor hangs in

Monument Park at Yankee Stadium. Maris became one of the few baseball players to appear on a postage stamp when the U.S. Postal Service issued its "Roger Maris, 61 in '61" stamp in 1999. Billy Crystal's movie *61** about the home run race premiered in 2001, half a century after the event. The movie's tagline was "Mickey Mantle and Roger Maris. Why did America have room in its heart for just one hero?"

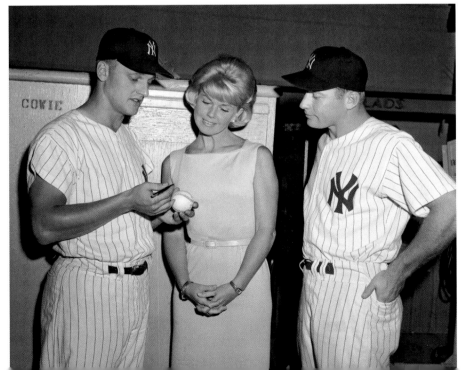

ABOVE: Roger Maris in full-flowing action for the Yankees in September 1960.

LEFT: Taking time out from their home run battle in August 1961, Roger Maris and Mickey Mantle chat with Doris Day on the set of *That Touch of Mink*. Along with Yogi Berra, they made several cameo appearances in other films.

ABOVE: Crooner Perry Como puts a reassuring arm on Mickey Mantle's shoulder as they rehearse for an appearance on *The Perry Como Show* in October 1961.

BELOW: The Kid meets the Babe. Six-year-old film star Jackie Coogan meets with Babe Ruth and Yankees owner Jacob Ruppert before a game at Yankee Stadium on April 14, 1921. Coogan later played Uncle Fester on the television series *The Addams Family*.

CELEBRITY FANS
The stars who love the Yankees

ABOVE: Singing duo Paul Simon and Art Garfunkel pose for a picture at Yankee Stadium on April 16, 1969, with Simon about to throw the ceremonial first pitch. He wrote about his first-ever visit to Yankee Stadium, when he was seven, in the *New York Times* in 2008: "We were playing the Indians and DiMaggio was returning to the lineup after an injury. As he approached the plate, the crowd was thumping. At the crack of the bat,

everyone around me stood to watch the ball's trajectory. I couldn't see a thing. It was a home run. I stood on my seat as Joe rounded third." Simon's song "Mrs. Robinson," which mentions DiMaggio, was a *Billboard* chart-topper in 1968, and the duo were given permission to film a video at Yankee Stadium. During the shoot, Garfunkel pitched to Simon, who wanted to test out his left-handed swing against the fabled "short porch" in

right field. When he finally connected with a pitch, the ball landed a disappointing 250 feet from home plate. The song reference to Joe DiMaggio has been interpreted as harking back to a simpler time when heroes could be relied upon. Ironically, Simon's baseball hero was Mickey Mantle, who appeared, playing stickball, in a video for a 1988 rerelease of the 1972 single "Me and Julio Down by the Schoolyard."

ABOVE: Matthew Broderick and wife Sarah Jessica Parker wave to the crowd from the back of a car in the Canyon of Heroes motorcade on October 30, 2000, celebrating the World Series victory. Parker is most famous for her role in the New York–based sitcom *Sex and the City*.

BELOW: *Sopranos* actor James Gandolfini acknowledges the crowd after reading Lou Gehrig's retirement speech as part of Project ALS (Lou Gehrig's disease) Day in Yankee Stadium on June 1, 2002.

ABOVE: Over forty years later, Paul Simon stands while watching a Yankees vs. Red Sox game at Yankee Stadium on July 29, 2012. Simon had participated in the unveiling of the monument to DiMaggio in April 1999, experiencing an emotional moment when the crowd sang, "Where have you gone, Joe DiMaggio?" He is one of many stars to have thrown the ceremonial first pitch at Yankees games; others include Alec Baldwin, Richard Gere, Jack Nicholson, Denzel Washington, Kate Hudson, Adam Sandler, and Cameron Diaz.

LEFT: Billy Crystal jogs with Derek Jeter during spring training in Tampa, Florida, in March 2008. Crystal was the driving force behind the movie *61*, which dramatized the home run battle between Maris and Mantle in 1961.

The Yankee DECADES
1970–1980

If the 1960s had ended as a dry spell, then the early 1970s continued the drought. It appeared that nothing the Yankees tried, both on and off the field, had much of an effect. Changing the managers, owners, and eventually the stadium altered little, and the Yankees were still trying to recapture former glories. The period from 1965 to 1975 was known as the Yankees' "lost years."

Yet the Yankees' prospects should have improved toward the end of the previous decade, following a restructuring of the American League. Having operated as a single division of 10 teams for years,

the league was split into two in 1969 with the East and West Divisions, both containing six teams. The Yankees, a founding member of the league, were in the same division as the Baltimore Orioles, Boston Red Sox, Cleveland Indians, Washington Senators, and Detroit Tigers, and finished fifth in 1969. Although they rallied and hauled themselves into second place in 1970, it was still a step down from the heady days of just 10 years ago.

The next three seasons epitomized the Yankees of the era: three straight fourth-place finishes,

proving that while CBS may have possessed big pockets, they had little idea of how to run a baseball team. In 1973 a group of investors headed by Cleveland-based shipbuilder George Steinbrenner concluded a deal with CBS that saw control of the club change hands for $8.7 million. By now Yankee Stadium was in desperate need of renovation or a complete overhaul, something even CBS had recognized, but their plans to renovate while the team would share the New York Mets' Shea Stadium had floundered when the Mets refused permission. Another plan called for a completely new stadium to be built in New

LEFT: The inimitable Ron Guidry, who broke many pitching records with the Yankees. In 1978 his 248 strikeouts broke the 74-year-old record set by Jack Chesbro.

RIGHT: Billy Martin and George Steinbrenner at a press conference in 1978; theirs was perhaps the most volatile relationship in baseball.

Jersey, at the Meadowlands, but eventually a compromise was found whereby the mayor of New York announced the city would buy Yankee Stadium for $24 million and lease it back to the club upon completion of the renovations in 1976. In the meantime, Shea Stadium, which was also owned by the city, would be made available to the Yankees despite the Mets' views on the matter.

In September 1973 came another major change as Ralph Houk resigned as manager after seven years in charge. In his place came Bill Virdon, whose single season as manager saw the Yankees playing at Shea Stadium. The new surroundings and new leadership did, at the very least, steer the Yankees in the right direction, but they nevertheless finished second in the division. After that season, George Steinbrenner began to make wholesale changes, signing star pitcher Jim "Catfish" Hunter from Oakland. Midway through the next season he brought in Billy Martin as manager for the first of Martin's numerous spells in charge of the team. Slowly the team made progress, but coupled with their return to Yankee Stadium, it appeared to be business as usual. A 97-win season in 1976 saw them top the East Division and then beat the Kansas City Royals in the American League Championship Series; Chris Chambliss hit a ninth-inning home run to secure a 3–2 victory and the team's 30th league pennant. The World Series was lost in six games to the Los Angeles Dodgers, but the fact that the Yankees made it to the series was indicative of how much Steinbrenner and his consortium had turned things around.

The following year they went one better, signing free agent Reggie Jackson to a five-year contract. The move paid dividends when the Yankees defeated the Royals in the playoffs and then extracted their revenge on the Dodgers in the World Series, with Reggie Jackson hitting three home runs in game six.

In 1978 there was a sense of déjà vu; the Yankees beat the Royals 3–1 in the playoffs, and the Dodgers fell in six games in the World Series. Ron Guidry, who would spend his entire career with the Yankees, set a record by striking out 18 batters in a 4–0 win against the California Angels at Yankee Stadium in June 1978. At the end of the season Guidry had posted a 25–3 record, a win percentage among the highest in baseball history, and enough to earn him the Cy Young Award.

That final year of the decade saw the Yankees suffer a number of losses. The East Division pennant slipped by, with the Yankees relegated to fourth place, denying them a third consecutive World Series. Far worse, however, was the loss of team captain Thurman Munson, who died in a plane crash in Canton, Ohio, on August 2, 1979. The entire team flew to Canton four days later for Munson's funeral, returning to New York later in the day for a game against the Baltimore Orioles. On that emotional day, the Yankees honored Munson by retiring his number 15 in a pregame ceremony.

BELOW: Reggie Jackson in full flow at Yankee Stadium in 1977.

THE LAST DAYS OF THE OLD YANKEE STADIUM

ABOVE: A little piece of history makes its way out of the stadium on September 30, 1973.

Yankee Stadium, the cathedral of baseball, was the sport's most magnificent and largest venue. By the mid-1960s, however, the imposing triple-decked structure had been allowed to deteriorate; by the early 1970s, it was urgently in need of renovation. The surrounding Bronx neighborhood was in decline and the Yankees' form was failing; the team suffered a World Series drought from 1962 to 1976.

CBS, which owned the team, proposed to undertake the renovation of the stadium in 1971, but the plans fell through when the New York Mets refused to allow the Yankees to share Shea Stadium. Two years later the city, led by Mayor John Lindsay, purchased Yankee Stadium and leased it back to the team. This time the Mets, also tenants of the city, had no option but to allow their local rivals to share Shea Stadium for two seasons, 1974 and 1975. An expansion team that had only joined the National League in 1962, the Mets were temporarily more successful than the Yankees.

Yankee Stadium closed on September 30, 1973. The Yankees lost the final game in the original stadium 8–5 to the Detroit Tigers. The last home run in the original stadium was hit by catcher Duke Sims, a former Tiger who had been with the Yankees for only a week. After the game, fans pried seats from the concrete to take home as souvenirs. The Yankees would later hold a "fire sale" of stadium memorabilia. Uncertainty lingered after manager Ralph Houk chose the day to announce his resignation; his intended rebuilding of the team was far from complete.

The season ended with the Yankees in fourth place with an 80–82 record, 17 games behind the Baltimore Orioles, who won the World Series that year. For Yankee fans, Shea Stadium in Queens was forbidden territory. Nevertheless, they followed their idols there during two years of exile.

Before the opening game at the refurbished Yankee Stadium on April 15, 1976, an on-field ceremony took place with Yankees legends Joe DiMaggio, Mickey Mantle, Whitey Ford, Yogi Berra, Billy Martin, Elston Howard, and Don Larsen all in attendance. The widows of Babe Ruth and Lou Gehrig also appeared. The first pitch in the renovated ballpark was thrown by 85-year-old Bob Shawkey, the starting pitcher in the first game played in the original stadium. It was a triumphant homecoming as the Yankees beat the Minnesota Twins 11–4 in front of 54,000 fans.

Plastic seats were installed in place of the original wooden ones. Suspension cables were installed in the upper decks, allowing the 118 steel columns supporting the roof and upper deck to be removed, greatly improving the view for spectators. An additional ten rows were added to the upper deck, which was cantilevered over the lower deck. Although some fans bemoaned the loss of tradition when the original stadium was dismantled, the Yankees' return home coincided with a welcome improvement on the field.

BELOW: A highly prized item for any Yankees fan: home plate.

BELOW: The exterior of the stadium as it looked in August 1973, prior to Old Timers' Day and an MLB game against Oakland A's.

YANKEES FANS CELEBRATE A WORLD SERIES

Today it's a given that World Series winners will get a ticker-tape parade. This wasn't always the case.

LEFT: Ticker-tape parades date back as far as 1886, and have celebrated not only athletes but also returning astronauts, politicians, and visiting dignitaries. The Yankees received their first in the spring of 1961, honoring their American League pennant of the previous year, when they'd lost the World Series to the Pittsburgh Pirates. None of their earlier triumphs, including five straight World Series titles from 1949 to 1953, had been given the ticker-tape treatment. Later in 1961, the Yankees beat the Cincinnati Reds in the World Series, and a parade was held in April 1962—but surprisingly, there was no parade for the 1962 World Series victory. Subsequent parades, when they happened, were held in October or November, shortly after the World Series. In October 1977, the Yankees' first World Series win in 15 years choked the streets of New York, as fans came out to cheer (pictured left). The newspaper headlines exclaimed "Reggie! Reggie! Reggie!" after Reggie Jackson hit three home runs in the final game to take the title.

RIGHT: Better late than never: Yogi Berra missed out on parades for all his World Series wins, but in 2009, accompanied by his wife Carmen, he got to ride in an open-top limousine during the Yankees' World Series victory parade.

ABOVE: On October 30, 2000, the Yankees celebrated their third consecutive World Series triumph. Part of the motorcade is seen here making its way along Broadway. The festivities were led by New York mayor Rudolph Giuliani, a longtime Yankees fan. More than a million people lined the route to watch the parade.

RIGHT: Derek Jeter greets fans lined up along the "Canyon of Heroes" on lower Broadway during the 2009 parade.

Thurman Munson

The Thurman Munson legend was created in four short years, beginning in 1976, when he was appointed the first captain of the Yankees since the immortal Lou Gehrig, to August 2, 1979, when he perished in a plane crash in Canton, Ohio.

Born in Akron, Ohio, on June 7, 1947, Thurman Munson was a one-team man. After being selected as the fourth pick of the 1968 Major League Baseball draft, he began his career with two seasons in the minor leagues, hitting over .300 in both. He did so again in 1970, his first full season as starting catcher, earning the American League Rookie of the Year Award with his .302 average. He won successive Gold Glove Awards in 1973, 1974, and 1975.

Munson's elevation to the captaincy in 1976 coincided with the Yankees' first American League pennant in 12 years, though they lost to the Cincinnati Reds in the World Series. The success was no coincidence, of course, as his American League MVP status underlined, and he went on to captain the Yankees to the World Series in 1977 and 1978. His personal stats were impressive: the 1977 season saw him achieve an average of .300 and drive in 100 runs for the third consecutive season—the first in the American League since 1954, and the first Yankee player to achieve the feat since Joe DiMaggio.

Munson's three World Series (1976, 1977, and 1978) saw him hit .529, .320, and .320 respectively, for an overall World Series average of .373. His career batting average was .292.

He put his influence on the team behind the plate well above his batting abilities. "I like hitting fourth and I like the good batting average. But what I do every day behind the plate is a lot more important because it touches so many more people and so many more aspects of the game."

"Thurman was one of the things you could always count on," said Yankees manager Billy Martin of the man who was a seven-time All-Star in 1971 and from 1973 to 1978. The man himself confessed that "I'm a little too belligerent. I cuss and swear at people. I yell at umpires and maybe I'm a little too tough at home sometimes."

He was as dedicated a family man as he was a hard-nosed professional. Munson lost his life practicing takeoffs and landings in an eight-seater plane he had bought to make it easier to see his wife and children on days he wasn't playing. It was rumored that Munson had thought about playing for the Cleveland Indians so he could be closer to home. True or not, the Yankees' sixth-ever team captain remained a Yankee to the end. He was just 32 years old and in the prime of his life.

The life, career, and memory of Thurman Munson was celebrated before the Yankees' next game, against the Baltimore Orioles. Only eight players took the field, catcher Jerry Narron remaining in the dugout. After a prayer and the singing of "America the Beautiful," the stadium erupted with an eight-minute chant of "Thurman! Thurman!" in tribute to the Yankees' fallen hero.

He has a plaque in Monument Park, the inscription for which was written by Yankees owner George Steinbrenner, an indication of the esteem in which he was held. When the new Yankee Stadium was built in 2009, Munson's locker, frozen in time, was transferred to the museum there. Munson's number 15 jerseys remain popular among Yankee fans, a reminder of a fallen hero whose spirit still soars.

ABOVE LEFT: Thurman Munson tags out second baseman Frank White of the Kansas City Royals during a 1978 game at Yankee Stadium.

ABOVE: Munson congratulates Rich Gossage after a Yankee win. Munson was one of the eleven Yankee captains nominated by the club since 1910.

★ **As if driven by the memory of their departed** captain, the Yankees blasted their way through the 1980 season, winning 103 games, with Reggie Jackson hitting .300 to go with 41 home runs. The team then stalled in the American League Championship Series, losing 3–0 to the Kansas City Royals; there would be no World Series to honor Thurman Munson. Free agent Dave Winfield was picked up in December 1980,

signing a then-record 10-year contract with the Yankees, proof that the owners were prepared to push the boat out in their acquisition of players. Unfortunately, the 1981 season was to be punctuated by a strike, instigated in part over the ongoing issue of compensation for free agents. The Yankees had managed to amass a 34–22 record before the strike was called, tops in the East Division.

As it would be impossible to complete the full season around the strike, a compromise was organized, with the season split into two halves; the team that finished atop the East Division in the first half (the Yankees) met the team that finished in first in the second half (the Milwaukee Brewers) to decide who would then progress into the ALCS. The Yankees beat the Brewers 3–2 and moved on to face the Oakland Athletics, sweeping them 3–0. Unfortunately, the season ended in disappointment when the Los Angeles Dodgers won the World Series 4–2.

That would turn out to be the Yankees' last visit to the World Series for 15 years, their longest playoff drought since the 1920s and their longest run without a World Series title since the 1910s. The lack of success came as a surprise, for the Yankees were still prepared to spend big on player acquisitions, both free agents and draft picks, but few of the players that were signed performed as anticipated.

With the players underperforming, pressure mounted on the manager, a virtual swinging-door policy coming into force during the early course of the decade. Bob Lemon joined for his second stint as manager in September 1981, being replaced nine months later by Gene Michael. Michael lasted barely four months before being replaced in turn by Clyde King, who would also be unable to revive the Yankees' fortunes.

In July 1983 the team featured in what would become known as the "Pine Tar Game" against the Kansas City Royals. The Royals' George Brett hit a two-out, ninth-inning home run off Goose Gossage to apparently give the Royals a 5–4 lead. Yankees manager Billy Martin noticed that Brett's bat contained a significant amount of pine tar, and requested that the umpires inspect the bat. The umpires eventually ruled that the homer was nullified because the pine tar on the bat exceeded the allowable 18 inches and called Brett out, which resulted in a 4–3 victory for the Yankees. The Royals protested the ruling all the way up to American League president Lee MacPhail (son of Larry), who upheld the protest and ordered that the game be restarted from the point of the home run. The Royals won it 5–4.

The rest of the decade was effectively a case of "so near and yet so far." Successive second-place finishes in 1985 and 1986 were the best the

Yankees could post in the 1980s, with several players also reaching the end of their careers. Ron Guidry began to suffer a succession of arm problems during the 1985 season soon after posting a 22–6 record, resulting in a drastic decline in his performance. Dennis Rasmussen won 18 games in 1986 but struggled to equal that record in subsequent years, while Rick Rhoden won 16 games in 1987 following his arrival from the Pirates but struggled to 14–14 a year later.

The changes were just as constant off the field, with Billy Martin being replaced by Yogi Berra in 1984, only to return again in 1985. His record during his fourth time in charge would prove to be the best of his Yankees career; his team won 91 of the 145 games in which he was in charge, for a winning percentage of .628, but it wasn't enough to get the Yankees to the top of the division and back into the World Series. Martin served one final turn as manager, replacing Lou Piniella (who had replaced Martin in 1986) in 1987, although this time around he could post only a .588 winning percentage over the course of 68 games.

LEFT: Always a controversial figure, arguing with fans, players, officials, and even Chicago cab drivers, Billy Martin once stated, "I may not have been the greatest Yankee to have put on the uniform, but I am the proudest." Astonishingly, he was being lined up to take over the Yankees for a sixth time for the 1990 season, but was killed in a car crash on Christmas Day in 1989 while working as a special consultant for George Steinbrenner. He was buried in the same cemetery as Babe Ruth. Former U.S. president Richard Nixon was among those who attended his funeral.

FAR LEFT AND BOTTOM: The pine tar argument and the measurement at home plate.

BELOW: Free agent Dave Winfield signed for ten years and $13 million from the San Diego Padres.

Don Mattingly

"Donnie Baseball," as Don Mattingly was affectionately known to the Yankee faithful, was an unlikely star. In the 1980s, which was a dark period for the Yankees, the first baseman stood out like a shining light. His nickname was coined by Minnesota Twins outfielder Kirby Puckett, one of many adversaries who was forced to grudgingly respect his drive, dedication, and never-say-die spirit—attributes that set him apart from average players.

Born in Indiana on April 20, 1961, Mattingly was drafted in the 19th round of the 1979 amateur draft. It was hardly the highest profile of entries, but the 175-pound six-footer belied his average physique—not to mention a lack of power and speed—to become a Yankee great.

While the team he played for remained infuriatingly unable to bring titles to Yankee Stadium, Mattingly appeared in the All-Star Game six times, won nine Gold Glove Awards, three Silver Slugger Awards, and was the American League's Most Valuable Player in 1985.

Mattingly's peak came in the late 1980s, a period when players who could hit .300 were scarce. He established himself with the Yankees in 1984, two years after his major league debut, thanks to the trade of Steve Balboni to Kansas City. That year he beat teammate Dave Winfield in a close race for the American League batting title. He was the game's top hitter, and could be relied upon for 25 to 30 home runs a season.

His 1985 total of 145 RBIs was the highest single-season total of the decade, while the following season his .350 average with 30 home runs was the best in the major leagues in 25 years. All but one of the six seasons from

1984 to 1989 saw him register 100 runs, while his total of 684 RBIs was 59 more than his nearest challenger, George Bell. In 1987 Mattingly tied Dale Long's major league record by hitting home runs in eight consecutive games, and set a major league record by hitting six grand slams in a season (both records have since been matched). These grand slams were the only six of his career.

Mattingly's defensive qualities won him the first of his nine Gold Glove Awards in 1985. Interestingly, he played games at second and third base early in his career, even though he was left-handed. He seldom complained. "I never felt I was as talented as some other players, but I was willing to try some things other players weren't willing to do. I played from the heart."

The 1990s proved a patchier affair for Mattingly, and back problems reduced his effectiveness. Even so, he managed a last golden season in 1995, hitting .417 in the postseason, the Yankees' only playoff appearance in his career, only to lose to Seattle. He sat out the following season due to an injury, and then retired. The Yankees retired his number 23, honoring a 14-year career served with one club. He finished his career with 2,153 hits, 222 home runs, 1,099 RBI, and a .307 lifetime average.

In 1992 Mattingly's iconic status was confirmed when he appeared in an episode of *The Simpsons* entitled "Homer at the Bat." Two of Mattingly's three sons attempted to follow in his footsteps, but their professional careers were short.

His major regret was not reaching the World Series—which, ironically, the Yankees did in 1996, the first year after his retirement. "I would have liked to experience it if it had come at a different time. The first year it was tough to watch because there were a lot of the same guys I played with. But when you get back to the basics, I wouldn't trade the memories I've had with the kids for World Series rings or any amount of money."

Don Mattingly returned to Yankee Stadium in 2004 to link with manager Joe Torre as the team's hitting coach and then bench coach, following Torre to the Dodgers in 2008 and succeeding him there as manager in 2011.

Mattingly is widely considered as the best Yankee player never to have played in a World Series. As a first baseman, he ranks behind Lou Gehrig as the pick of the Yankees' bunch. His plaque in Monument Park at Yankee Stadium, dedicated in August 1997, calls him "a humble man of grace and dignity, a captain who led by example, proud of the pinstripe tradition and dedicated to the pursuit of excellence, a Yankee forever."

ABOVE: Don Mattingly stands at home plate watching the flight of a home run clear the fence at Yankee Stadium in 1986.

BELOW: Mattingly in action during the 1993 season, catching a pop-up fly at first base. Don was the Yankees' captain from 1991 until his retirement in 1995.

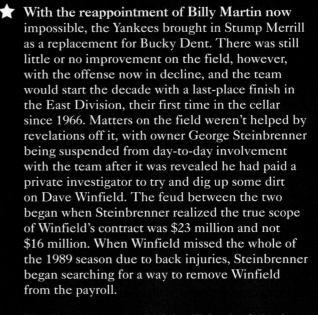

With the reappointment of Billy Martin now impossible, the Yankees brought in Stump Merrill as a replacement for Bucky Dent. There was still little or no improvement on the field, however, with the offense now in decline, and the team would start the decade with a last-place finish in the East Division, their first time in the cellar since 1966. Matters on the field weren't helped by revelations off it, with owner George Steinbrenner being suspended from day-to-day involvement with the team after it was revealed he had paid a private investigator to try and dig up some dirt on Dave Winfield. The feud between the two began when Steinbrenner realized the true scope of Winfield's contract was $23 million and not $16 million. When Winfield missed the whole of the 1989 season due to back injuries, Steinbrenner began searching for a way to remove Winfield from the payroll.

The Yankees stuck with Merrill for the following season, but the improvement was only marginal, the team hoisting themselves up to fifth in the division. Merrill was replaced in 1992 by Buck Showalter, who would go on to lay down the foundations for a more gradual improvement. Guided by Showalter and general manager Gene Michael, the Yankees switched emphasis from buying talent to building up the farm system, developing their own players and then holding on to the top performers who came through. They appeared to have turned the corner during the 1994 season, posting the best record in the American League before the season was brought to an abrupt halt thanks to another players' strike. The strike was all the worse for the club, since the Yankees had been expected to reach the World Series that season.

Fortunately, the progress made in 1994 continued into 1995 when the strike was over. The Yankees finished second in the East Division and reached the playoffs as a wild card. Despite winning the first two games of the Division Series against the Seattle Mariners, the Yankees were beaten 3–2 to bring Don Mattingly's dream of a World Series with the Yankees to an end—he had joined the team in 1982, a year after their last appearance, and would retire in 1995.

Despite the strides Showalter had made, it was time for a new manager. Joe Torre was hired for the position, along with Don Zimmer as his bench coach and former Yankees pitcher Mel Stottlemyre as the pitching coach. It all clicked into place in 1996, with the Yankees ending their 18-year dry spell by reclaiming the World Series. After winning the East Division, the Yankees beat the Texas Rangers 3–1 in the ALDS and then the Baltimore Orioles 4–1 in the ALCS. Despite losing the first two games at home by a combined score of 16–1, the Yankees recovered to win the series in six games; Derek Jeter topped a superb season by being named Rookie of the Year. Another outstanding performer among many was center fielder Bernie Williams, a Yankee favorite from 1991 to 2006.

If the success was to be maintained, there would have to be subtle changes to the team, with lefties David Wells and Mike Stanton being brought in to bolster the pitching staff. Despite the acquisitions, the team lost the 1997 ALDS to the Cleveland Indians 3–2, but this was to be only a temporary fall from grace. The following season, the Yankees posted one of the greatest performances in the history of the game, going through the regular season with a 114–48 record, a phenomenal .704 winning percentage. The Texas Rangers were swept in the ALDS, and then the Cleveland Indians were beaten 4–2 in the ALCS to ensure the Yankees a place in the World Series. There the Yankees captured the championship with a sweep of the San Diego Padres; it was 24th World Series title in club history.

The decade ended with the World Series being retained. Although the Yankees' 98 wins in the regular season was not as commanding as the

year before—then again, few could have expected anyone to equal that 1998 record—the Texas Rangers and the Boston Red Sox proved no match in the ALDS and ALCS, being beaten 3–0 and 4–1, respectively. Up against the Yankees in the World Series were the Atlanta Braves, the same team the Yankees had beaten in 1996.

It was to be another sweep, a victory that also set a little bit of history, for it was to be the last time the Yankees won the World Series at Yankee Stadium. In addition to winning the World Series, they posted an impressive 22–3 postseason record, including four series sweeps, over the course of two years. It was an impressive record, one that went a long way to confirm the Yankees' return to reeminence in baseball and also that Joe Torre was far from "Clueless Joe." He was on his way to becoming one of the team's—if not the game's—greatest managers.

FAR LEFT: Derek Jeter turns a double play over the Atlanta Braves' Marquis Grissom during game three of the World Series at Fulton County Stadium in Atlanta, Georgia, on October 22, 1996.

LEFT: The Yankees' Bernie Williams runs the bases in a game against the Oakland Athletics in July 1991.

BELOW: Not for the first time, observers were far from impressed with a new manager. The *New York Post* derided Joe Torre as "Clueless Joe" (a play on "Shoeless Joe" Jackson), but over the next 11 years, Torre proved to be one of the most successful managers in the team's history.
.

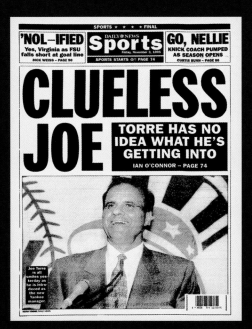

THE YANKEES ARE CROWNED WORLD CHAMPIONS AFTER AN 18-YEAR DROUGHT

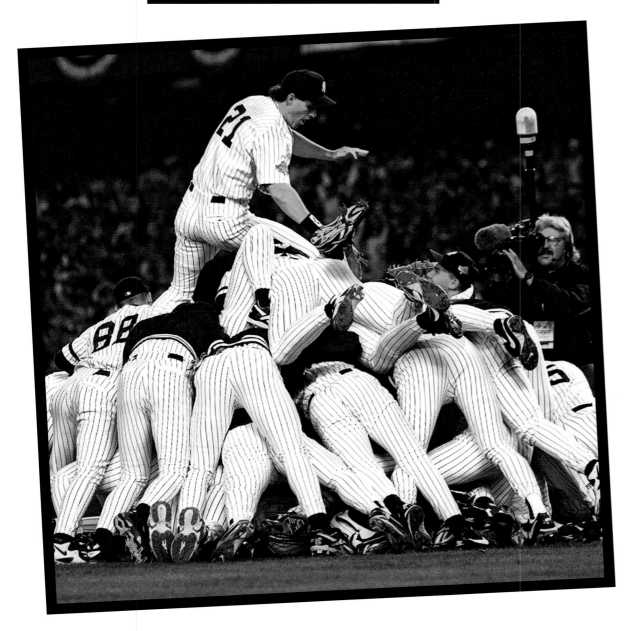

LEFT: Paul O'Neill leaps on top of the pile of celebrating players after the Yankees clinch the World Series.

The 1996 season got off to a difficult start for new Yankees manager Joe Torre. Buck Showalter had been dismissed in 1995, partly for losing in the playoffs and partly because of the aftereffects of the 1994 players' strike. Torre was a veteran manager, having held the position with the New York Mets, Atlanta Braves, and St. Louis Cardinals. He had been out of work since being fired by the Cardinals in June 1995.

The prestigious Yankees managerial job could also be a poisoned chalice; owner George Steinbrenner had a well-earned reputation for impatience; 21 managers had come and gone in 23 seasons. Torre knew that he was not Steinbrenner's first choice, but it didn't bother him. He was determined to show what he could do. Initially, he was ridiculed by the press as being too old at 55, having a career losing record of 894–1,003, and not a single postseason victory to his name.

Fans were also skeptical about Torre, but he shrugged doubters aside and, along with the team's management, set about strengthening the roster by signing players such as Joe Girardi, Tino Martinez, Jeff Nelson, Mariano Duncan, Kenny Rogers, and Wade Boggs.

Unlike some of the great Yankees teams, the class of 1996 was not dominated by big-name players, there were no prodigious home run feats, and no record-breaking statistics to power their pursuit of glory, although shortstop Derek Jeter, who hit a home run on the first day of the season at Cleveland, was clearly a star in the making. Neither the defense nor the offense was outstanding, but by teamwork and persistence they ground out victories, never losing more than five consecutive games. They capitalized on other teams' errors and weaknesses.

Although Steinbrenner was reportedly unhappy with his team's style of play, the Yankees won their first division title since 1981, finishing with a 92–70 record, four games ahead of the Baltimore Orioles. A 3–1 victory over the Texas Rangers in the American League Division Series was followed by taking the American League Championship Series with a 4–1 win over the Baltimore Orioles, who had claimed the wild card. The Yankees were on their way to their first appearance in the Fall Classic for 15 years.

The Bronx Bombers' opponents, the Atlanta Braves, were strong favorites for the world title. Games one and two were rescheduled because of heavy rain in New York, and the Yankees lost both games. Afterward, Steinbrenner held crisis talks with Torre, who assured the skeptical owner that the Yankees would win all three games in Atlanta.

New York pulled off the first part of this daunting task in game three thanks to a superb pitching performance from David Cone, and Bernie Williams's two-run homer sealed the victory for the Yankees. In game four, the Yankees recovered from being down 6–0 at the top of the sixth inning to complete one of the great comebacks in World Series history, winning 8–6 to even the series. Torre made good on his promise when New York won game five 1–0; it was a tight affair decided by an unearned run, sending the series back to the Big Apple. This was a nervous affair, with plenty of tense moments for Yankee fans.

New York took a 3–0 lead in the third inning and held on to win 3–2, ending their 18-year world championship drought and becoming the only team to win the World Series after losing the first two games at home. The victory sparked scenes of wild celebration inside Yankee Stadium, including Wade Boggs joining a police officer on horseback. It also represented vindication for the manager

who had won the prize in his first season. After this game, George Steinbrenner ripped up Torre's contract and rewarded him with a longer, more lucrative deal.

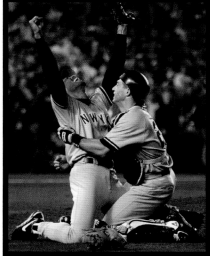

BELOW LEFT: Pitcher John Wetteland walks arm in arm with Joe Torre after the Yankees defeated the Atlanta Braves 3–2 in game six. Wetteland was named MVP of the series.

BELOW: Mariano Rivera sinks to his knees after the victory and is hugged by catcher Joe Girardi.

Derek Jeter ② 2

One of the most successful and popular baseball players in recent memory, Derek Jeter has been a fixture with the Yankees since making his major league debut as a 20-year-old in 1995.

Derek Jeter was born in Pequannock Township, New Jersey, on June 26, 1974. His parents insisted that he be brought up with a positive attitude, making him sign a yearly contract that set out standards of behavior that were expected of him. While certainly unorthodox, it had the desired effect. An all-around athlete, Jeter excelled at baseball and basketball at Kalamazoo Central High School in Michigan, although it was his exploits at baseball that attracted the most attention and awards, including the 1992 Gatorade High School Player of the Year Award.

By the time of the draft in 1992, Jeter was widely expected to go to the Houston Astros, who held the first pick. Perhaps believing that he would demand a hefty signing bonus, they passed on Jeter, prompting their scout to quit his job in protest. The Astros' loss proved to be the Yankees' gain, for when Jeter was still available with the sixth pick, they drafted him. He signed an $800,000 contract and turned professional.

Jeter would spend the next four seasons learning his trade in minor league baseball, eventually getting his break with the Yankees following injuries to Tony Fernandez and Pat Kelly early in the 1995 season. After initially struggling to adapt to the majors, Jeter eventually settled into the team and proved that all the acclaim and expectation was justified, collecting all 28 first-place votes for the American League Rookie of the Year Award in 1996. That was to be the first of many major honors heading his way, and he was subsequently selected for his first All-Star Game in 1998. He has since gone on to earn 13 more selections, missing only two years (2003 and 2005) for which he would have been eligible.

ABOVE: Jeter began the 1992 season with the Gulf Coast Yankees of the rookie-level Gulf Coast League.

BELOW: Jeter lies injured after fielding a grounder in the 12th inning of game one of the 2012 ALCS against the Detroit Tigers in Yankee Stadium.

These accolades have been received on the back of some strong performances for the Yankees, during which time Jeter has amassed the most hits (3,274), games played (2,543), stolen bases (346), and at bats (10,369) of any player since his first appearance in the major leagues in 1995.

His hitting ability, baserunning, and overall leadership have brought the Yankees five World Series titles, and he has also earned five Gold Glove Awards for himself. As age has continued its relentless march, Jeter has adapted his routine, spending more time at physical conditioning to ensure he is able to continue playing the game at the very peak of his abilities.

With success has come reward; he signed a $189 million contract in 2001 that was the second highest in all sports at the time. Despite the riches, Jeter has kept his feet very firmly on the ground, setting up the Turn 2 Foundation in 1996, which was established to help teenagers avoid drug and alcohol addiction, and to encourage those same teenagers to attain high levels of academic achievement.

Jeter swings at most pitches either in or near the strike zone. While right-handed hitters have a tendency to pull the ball into left field, his inside-out swing, known throughout the game as the "Jeterian swing," results in most of his hits going to center and right field. A large percentage of his home runs have been hit to right field rather than center or left field.

He is generally considered to be one of the most consistent players, having missed very few games during the course of his career (a dislocated shoulder in 2003 and a calf injury in 2011 resulted in him posting the only two seasons with less than 148 games played). This is fueled by his ongoing passion for the game and his overwhelming desire to win. "If you're going to play at all, you're out to win. Baseball, board games, playing Jeopardy, I hate to lose." Derek Jeter has not had many losses during the course of his career, as his record and awards confirm.

BELOW: Derek Jeter runs the bases after career hit number 3,000, a solo home run in the third inning against the Tampa Bay Rays at Yankee Stadium on July 9, 2011. He is the longest-serving Yankee captain, with 2013 marking his eleventh season in the role.

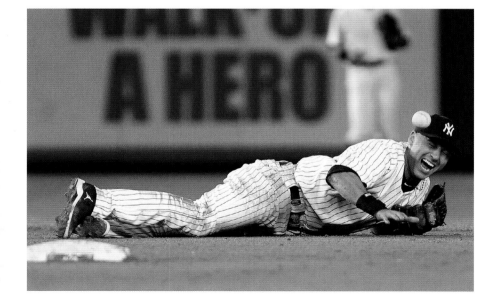

GAME CHANGERS
KEY MOMENTS IN YANKEE HISTORY

THE YANKEES WIN A RECORD 114 GAMES IN THE REGULAR SEASON

The 1997 season ended in disappointment for the Yankees; although finishing second in the American League East was enough to gain them a wild-card berth in the playoffs, they lost the Division Series to the Cleveland Indians. The off-season witnessed a flurry of transactions as manager Joe Torre and the Yankees' management sought to strengthen the team.

The key to the success of the 1998 roster was, like that of the class of 1996, teamwork. Every player knew his job and carried it out to the best of his ability. The personnel possessed a winning blend of youth and experience, power and skill, right- and left-handed pitching. The statistics show that the 1998 Yankees had different players leading in batting average, home runs, hits, total bases, and walks. But this was a group of men unconcerned with individual statistics; winning was all that mattered. It was another Yankees team hailed as the greatest of all time.

In a season where much attention was focused on the exploits of Mark McGwire and Sammy Sosa in chasing Roger Maris's record of 61 home runs, the Yankees forged a new dynasty with a team for which no player hit more than 28 homers.

The determination to win was evidenced in the franchise's record total of 114 wins. This set an American League record that stood until it was

LEFT: The Yankees' Mariano Rivera is mobbed by teammates after the final out in game four of the World Series against the San Diego Padres at Qualcomm Stadium in San Diego.

DAVID WELLS THROWS THE FIRST PERFECT GAME SINCE DON LARSEN

In a season characterized by team spirit, one individual feat stood out. On May 17, 1998, Yankees pitcher David Wells retired all 27 Minnesota Twins batters in a 4–0 win, completing the first perfect game by a Yankee since Don Larsen's back in 1956. It was the second perfect game and tenth no-hitter in Yankee history, and the first Yankee no-hitter since Dwight Gooden's against the Seattle Mariners in May 1996.

Wells completed the shutout with 120 pitches. Inside Yankee Stadium, 49,820 fans watched as the event unfolded over 2 hours and 40 minutes. The previous perfect game had been thrown four years earlier by Kenny Rogers of the Texas Rangers against the California Angels.

The Yankees became only the second franchise to have two perfect games, tying the record held by the Cleveland Indians. Yankee fans would only have to wait just over a year before David Cone added a third perfect game against the Montreal Expos in July 1999 at Yankee Stadium.

Wells signed as a free agent for the Yankees in 1997 after being a journeyman starter earlier in his career, which began with the Toronto Blue Jays in 1987. He came to be regarded as one of the best left-handed pitchers in the game. For the Yankees, he wore number 33 in honor of his hero, Babe Ruth. Coincidentally, he attended the same San Diego high school as Don Larsen. He was known as a big drinker and claimed in his autobiography to have been hung over when he pitched his perfect game. Four months later, he very nearly completed an unprecedented second perfect game against the Oakland A's, but gave up a run in the seventh inning. After retiring from baseball in 2007, he went into broadcasting.

topped by the Seattle Mariners' 116 wins in 2001. A postseason record of 11–2 established a new benchmark for total wins in the regular season and playoffs, surpassing the Mets' total of 116 in 1986.

That postseason saw the Bronx Bombers sweep the Texas Rangers 3–0 in the Division Series, during which they surrendered only one run and 13 hits. The American League Championship Series against Cleveland was a little more problematical, as the Yankees needed six games to close the deal. In the World Series, they swept the San Diego Padres after falling behind 5–2 in the seventh inning of the first game.

ABOVE: Chuck Knoblauch tosses his bat while watching the flight of his three-run home run against the San Diego Padres in the seventh inning of game one of the World Series in Yankee Stadium.

LEFT: Derek Jeter launches one in San Diego.

BELOW: Yankees manager Joe Torre.

★ **The Yankees would continue their streak of** success into the new century, never finishing below third place in the East Division in any season. Indeed, only one season has ever seen them finish outside of the wild-card position, that being a third-place finish in 2008. The new century began just the way the old one had ended, with the Yankees winning the World Series. After posting 87 wins in the regular season, the Yankees would beat the Oakland Athletics 3–2 in the ALDS and the Seattle Mariners 4–2 in the ALCS.

That brought up a clash with the New York Mets in the World Series, the so-called Subway Series, the first such series since the Yankees played the Brooklyn Dodgers 1956. After taking a 2–0 lead at home, the Yankees journeyed to Shea Stadium. Although the Mets claimed the third game, the Yankees finished off the series with two more victories on the road. The Yankees' victory marked the first time any visiting team had won a World Series at Shea Stadium. The Yankees were also the first team to have won three consecutive World Series since the Oakland Athletics achieved the feat in 1972, 1973, and 1974.

The Yankees had hoped to stretch that record to a fourth World Series in 2001, a year made all the more poignant by the events in New York on September 11. The ALDS was secured with a 3–2 win over the Oakland Athletics, followed by a 4–1 win over the Seattle Mariners. In the World Series they faced the Arizona Diamondbacks, who had been in existence for only four seasons. Arizona started well, winning the first two games, although the Yankees would go on to win the next three at Yankee Stadium, where President George W. Bush tossed the ceremonial first pitch before game three. The series returned to Arizona, where the Diamondbacks evened the series in game six and then captured the title with a 3–2 victory in the final game. Although the Yankees fell short of their goal, far more revealing was the fact that the Diamondbacks outscored the Yankees 37–14 over the course of the series.

There were to be further disappointments in the ensuing years, the next World Series not being won until 2009. There were occasions when the Yankees should have secured the title, most notably in 2004, but a collapse against the Boston Red Sox put an end to that campaign. After rushing into a 3–0 lead in the ALCS, the Yankees suffered one of the worst implosions in baseball history and lost the next four games.

Joe Torre would continue as manager of the Yankees until 2007, the longest tenure since Joe McCarthy. During that spell he oversaw the team through more than 1,150 victories and 13 consecutive postseason appearances. Despite his record, Torre was under severe pressure as the 2007 season came to a close, with George Steinbrenner announcing that Torre's contract would not be renewed if the Yankees failed to beat the Cleveland Indians. The Yankees lost 3–1, although Steinbrenner seemingly had a slight change of heart and did offer the popular manager a new contract.

Unfortunately, the terms effectively meant a pay cut, based as it was on a basic salary and incentives for winning the ALDS, ALCS, and World Series, with a further contract option if the Yankees captured the World Series. Although the contract would still ensure Joe Torre was the best-paid manager in baseball, most observers viewed it as insulting for a man who had achieved as much as Torre had during the course of his time in charge of the Yankees. Torre turned down the offer and walked away from the club where he had made not only his name but also created a new Yankees dynasty.

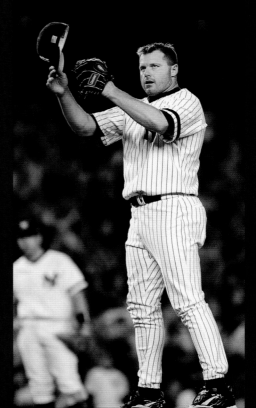

ABOVE: Pitcher Roger Clemens doffs his hat to the cheering fans after moving into third place on the all-time strikeout list in the fourth inning of a game against Tampa Bay at Yankee Stadium in September 2001.

LEFT: Alfonso Soriano (center) celebrates after his game-winning home run in a 3–1 victory over the Seattle Mariners in game four of the American League Championship Series at Yankee Stadium in 2001.

FAR LEFT: President George W. Bush gives the thumbs-up to the crowd before delivering the ceremonial first pitch at game three of the World Series on October 30, 2001.

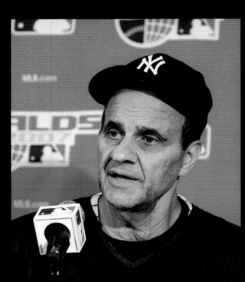

ABOVE: Joe Torre talks to the media after the Yankees defeated the Cleveland Indians 8–4 in game three of the American League Division Series at Yankee Stadium on October 7, 2007. It would be his last season in charge.

RIGHT: While the new season got underway in April 2010, demolition work continued on the old Yankee Stadium.

FAR RIGHT: After the final out of the 2009 World Series, Alex Rodriguez celebrates the Yankees' victory over Philadelphia.

OPPOSITE PAGE: Fighter jets fly overhead before the opening-day game against the Cleveland Indians at the new Yankee Stadium on April 16, 2009.

Torre's success, unrivaled in modern baseball, has made him a difficult man to follow. Just ask his successor Joe Girardi, who was appointed in 2008. Any result that is less than first place in the American League East is viewed as failure, and failure is not an option for the New York Yankees. A stuttering start to the 2008 campaign meant the Yankees had too much to do to top the league that season, which resulted in their missing the playoffs.

Fortunately for Girardi, the blip was a temporary one, as the Yankees returned to the top of the league in 2009 and won the ALDS 3–0 against the Minnesota Twins. The Los Angeles Angels of Anaheim were dispatched in the ALCS 4–2, ensuring that the Yankees were back in the World

Series after a six-year absence. In what was to be a fitting end to the team's first season at the new Yankee Stadium, the Yankees won their 27th title in 40 World Series appearances, beating the Philadelphia Phillies in six games.

Girardi has yet to lift the World Series trophy since that year. A wild card berth in 2010 saw the Yankees beat the Minnesota Twins 3–0 in the ALDS, but the Texas Rangers won the ALCS in six games. A year later the Yankees topped the division but lost the ALDS 3–2 to the Detroit Tigers. The Tigers were again the Yankees' nemesis in 2012, sweeping them in the ACLS, with Derek Jeter exiting the first game with a fractured ankle that would require surgery and months of rehabilitation. With mainstays such as Jeter, Alex Rodriguez, and Mariano Rivera heading toward the end of their careers, the Yankees' rebuilding begins again.

Mariano Rivera

The failed soccer player and failed shortstop is a religious man who believes his success as a pitcher was preordained. And many Yankee fans would subscribe to the idea that he has God-given talent.

Born in Panama City on November 29, 1969, he took to baseball at a very young age, fashioning milk cartons as gloves and tree branches as bats, making the balls by taping wads of shredded fishing nets and beat-up baseballs with electrical tape. With the make-do equipment, Rivera and his friends occupied much of their spare time playing baseball, although there were also frequent soccer games to break the routine. At one time he aspired to be a professional soccer player, but a succession of ankle injuries incurred while representing Pedro Pablo Sanchez High School put an end to those dreams.

Instead, Rivera reverted back to baseball, turning out for the amateur Panama Oeste team, where he was first spotted by Yankee scout Herb Raybourn. Although impressed with Rivera's performance, Raybourn did not see enough ability to warrant a professional contract—but fate was waiting to take a hand. Rivera switched to pitching after he performed badly at shortstop. He excelled as a pitcher, prompting his teammates to make contact with another Yankee scout and invite him to take a second look.

Two weeks later, Rivera was invited along to a tryout camp and, as luck would have it, Raybourn was in attendance. Having rejected the player as a shortstop, Raybourn was surprised to see Rivera pitching, but quickly spotted his raw talent; he promptly signed the amateur to a contract with a $3,000 signing bonus in February 1990.

Although unable to speak English and having never previously left home, Rivera began his professional career with the rookie-level Yankees of the Gulf Coast League. For the next five years he worked diligently at both his game and mastering the English language, with the improvement in his pitching velocity the most marked. Having previously thrown at 85 to 87 miles an hour when he first attended the tryout camp, within five years he had increased the velocity of his fastball to 95 miles an hour.

Having at one time considered trading Rivera to the Detroit Tigers, the Yankees had a change of mind when the statistics of his improvement on the mound were revealed. The cancellation of trading negotiations proved to be the virtual making of Rivera, and would later prompt a rival manager to state, "He needs to pitch in a higher league, if there is one. Ban him from baseball. He should be illegal."

That improvement, which Rivera claimed was given to him by God, resulted in the Yankees winning the World Series in 1996, their first title since 1978. He was further rewarded when the Yankees' management opted not to resign John

Wetteland in 1997, installing Rivera as the closer. After a disappointing 1997 season, he became one of the game's best closers in subsequent seasons, helping the Yankees win the World Series in 1998, 1999, 2000, and 2009. He would also earn 12 All-Star Game picks and be named Delivery Man of the Year on three occasions (2005, 2006, and 2009).

A deeply religious man, Rivera believes that everything that has happened to him during the course of his career is preordained. His pitching glove is inscribed "Phil. 4:13," which references the Biblical verse Philippians 4:13: "I can do all things through Christ, who strengthens me."

Like several of his teammates, Mariano Rivera has used his success and wealth to benefit others, making numerous donations to charities and foundations in his native Panama. Having already built an elementary school and church, the Mariano Rivera Foundation dispenses more than $500,000 annually to help underprivileged children in both the United States and Panama. Rivera has already stated that when his baseball career is at an end, he will concentrate on philanthropy, perhaps fitting for a man who is considered one of the most generous celebrities in the country.

ABOVE LEFT: Mariano Rivera playing stickball with children from his village of Puerto Caimito in Panama in February 1997.

ABOVE RIGHT: Rivera pitching against the Oakland Athletics in 1997. Rivera is regarded by many as one of the most dominant relievers in the history of the game.

YANKEES
THEN AND NOW

YANKEE STADIUM, ALMOST COMPLETE

The great stadiums before they opened

LEFT: Seen from a plane circling over the Bronx, the finishing touches are put on the original Yankee Stadium on April 1, 1923. In the early 1920s, the Bronx had yet to be developed and there was little industry along the Harlem River around 161st Street. Across the river, the horseshoe-shaped outline of the Polo Grounds appears in the top right corner of the photo.

RIGHT: Fast-forward to June 2008, and the new Yankee Stadium is going up alongside the old one. Owner George Steinbrenner had been agitating for a move out of the old ballpark for some years, even looking to move the team from its spiritual home in the Bronx. An agreement was finally reached with the city authorities in 2005, and construction began with a groundbreaking ceremony with Mayor Michael Bloomberg on August 16, 2006. The Yankees played on in the original stadium during the 2007 and 2008 seasons while its replacement took shape across the street. The new facility was closely modeled on the 1923 version, taking in features from before and after the 1970s refurbishment, including the limestone facade. The seating and field dimensions are similar to those of the old Yankee Stadium.

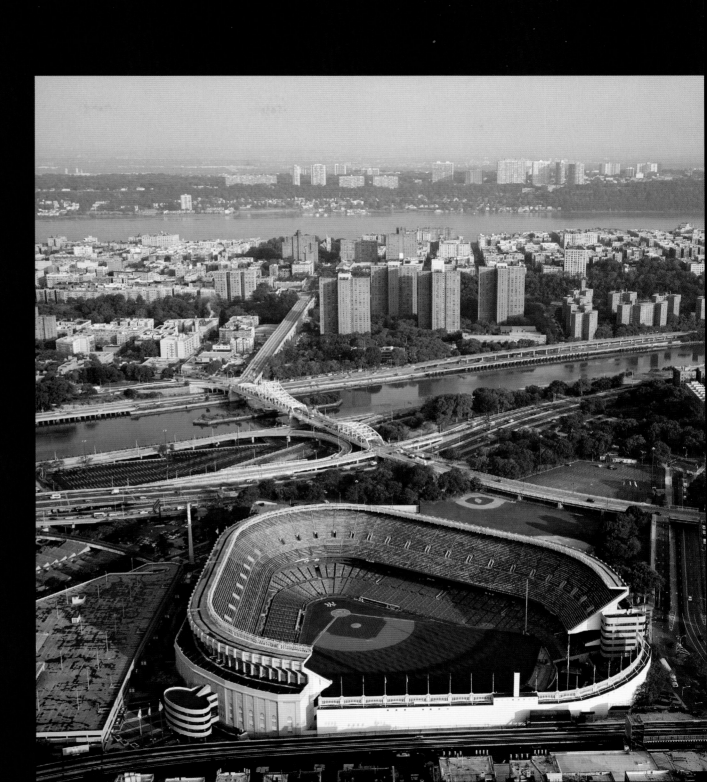

YANKEE STADIUM, ALMOST COMPLETE
Aerial views of the great stadiums before they opened

ABOVE: The same viewpoint in June 2008, with the new
Yankee Stadium rising next door to the original.

GAME CHANGERS

KEY MOMENTS IN YANKEE HISTORY

THE NEW YANKEE STADIUM OPENS IN 2009

ABOVE: Yogi Berra throws the ceremonial first pitch before the opening-day game between the Yankees and the Cleveland Indians.

Despite the extensive remodeling of the old Yankee Stadium in 1976, owner George Steinbrenner was already talking about the need for a new ballpark in the 1980s. He threatened to move the Yankees across the river to New Jersey because of the decaying conditions in the surrounding Bronx neighborhood. Negotiations began with the City of New York, and in the late 1990s, Mayor Rudolph Giuliani agreed to a deal that would have committed large amounts of public money to constructing a new stadium. This provoked controversy, leading Giuliani's successor, Michael Bloomberg, to invoke an escape clause, devising instead a new scheme under which the city would pay for transportation and infrastructure improvement and the franchise would fund the construction of the ballpark. The announcement of the building of a new stadium was made in June 2005.

Ironically, the site chosen was Macombs Dam Park, just across the street from the existing stadium, and formerly a public open space. The groundbreaking ceremony took place on August 16, 2006. The Bronx Bombers continued to play in the original stadium while the new one was being constructed. The project was disrupted when a construction worker and Red Sox devotee buried a replica Boston jersey beneath the visitors' dugout. His attempt to sabotage the new stadium in revenge for the Curse of the Bambino was unsuccessful, and he was forced to help dig up the jersey.

The new stadium was closely modeled on the original, retaining many of the iconic features; the dimensions of the field of play replicate those of the old in its final days. Because of the larger seats, the capacity was reduced by about 4,000 to 52,325. The Indiana limestone exterior closely resembles that of the old. The facade was re-created in the same position, along the upper deck of the grandstand, but it was no longer a purely decorative feature—it was now part of the support structure for the top deck and for the lighting above. Monument Park was moved to

behind the center-field fence, beneath a sports bar, which some fans criticized as inappropriate. The fact that Monument Park was no longer out in the open was also unpopular with many. Quite a few hardcore supporters were unhappy with the building of a new stadium, believing that the rich history of the original could have been preserved and that another refurbishment would have been the better option.

After a workout day in front of fans from the Bronx on April 2, the new Yankee Stadium hosted its first baseball game the next day when the Yankees faced the Chicago Cubs in an exhibition. The ceremonial first pitch was thrown by Reggie Jackson. On an emotional evening, the Yankees won 7–4. The official opening day was April 16, with a crowd of 48,271 in attendance to watch the game with the Cleveland Indians.

ABOVE: Yogi Berra greets Jose Molina out on the field after throwing the ceremonial first pitch. The cost of construction spiraled to $1.5 billion, making it the most expensive baseball stadium ever and the third most expensive stadium in the world, behind London's new Wembley Stadium and MetLife Stadium in East Rutherford, New Jersey.

LEFT: Former star pitchers Don Larsen and Whitey Ford take dirt from the pitcher's mound during an opening-day ceremony at the new Yankee Stadium on April 16, 2009.